Sally O. Lee's **Book of Illustrations**

I would like to thank my family and friends
for their love and support in helping
me to write and publish this book.

Library of Congress Control Number: 2015904327

For more information: visit www.sallyleebooks.com
Sally O. Lee's Book of Illustrations/ Sally O. Lee

Summary: This is a compilation of Sally O. Lee's illustrations.

ISBN-13: 978-1508846000

ISBN-10: 1508846006

This book is typeset in Garamond.
The illustrations are rendered in various mediums including watercolor,
pen and ink, pencil, pen and digital.

Printed in the U.S.A.

First Edition

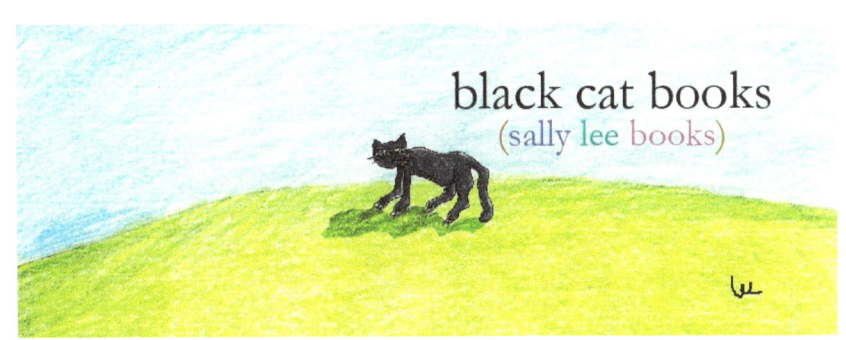

black cat books
(sally lee books)

Introduction:

I have been creating, drawing, painting, and illustrating for many, many moons. I have been storing my various works in boxes and on line. I have such a collection now, that I wanted to share my images with you.

Instead of titling each illustration separately, I will just say that this a compilation from various contest entries, submissions, my web site - sallyleebooks.com, among others. None of these have been published (except for *Santa's Glee* for Dana Farber) except for here and in my own work and on my web site. I like to consider some of these from my Salon de Refusés as many of these illustrations are rejections from various publications.

So get a cup of coffee and sit down and enjoy this book. I have had a lot of fun making these illustrations, and I hope you have just as much fun looking at them.

Cheers,

Sally Lee

To:

My yoga pals who teach me about love
every day.

And to my fluffy cat, Dominic. You
bring me so much joy, and I love you.

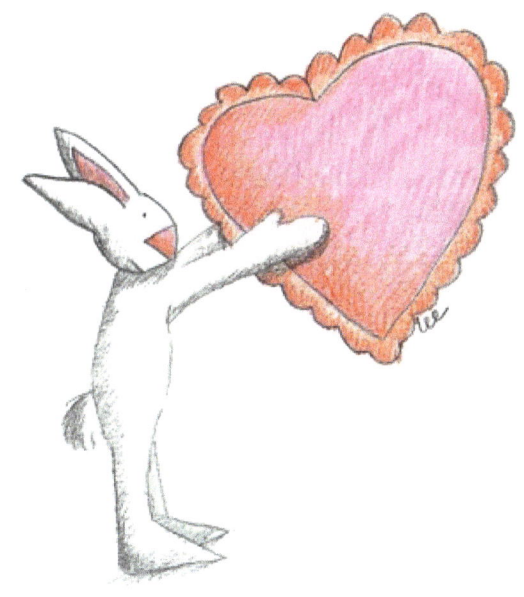

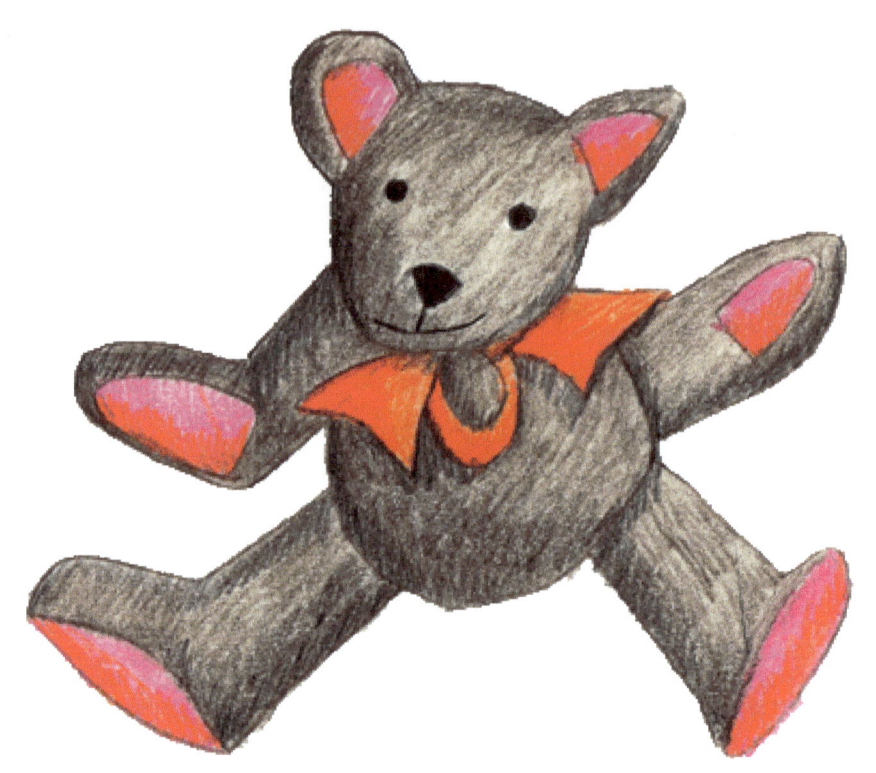

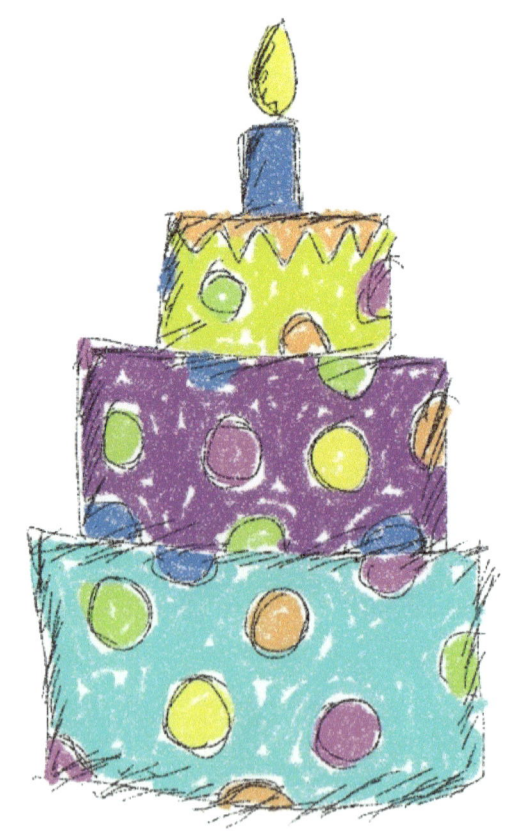

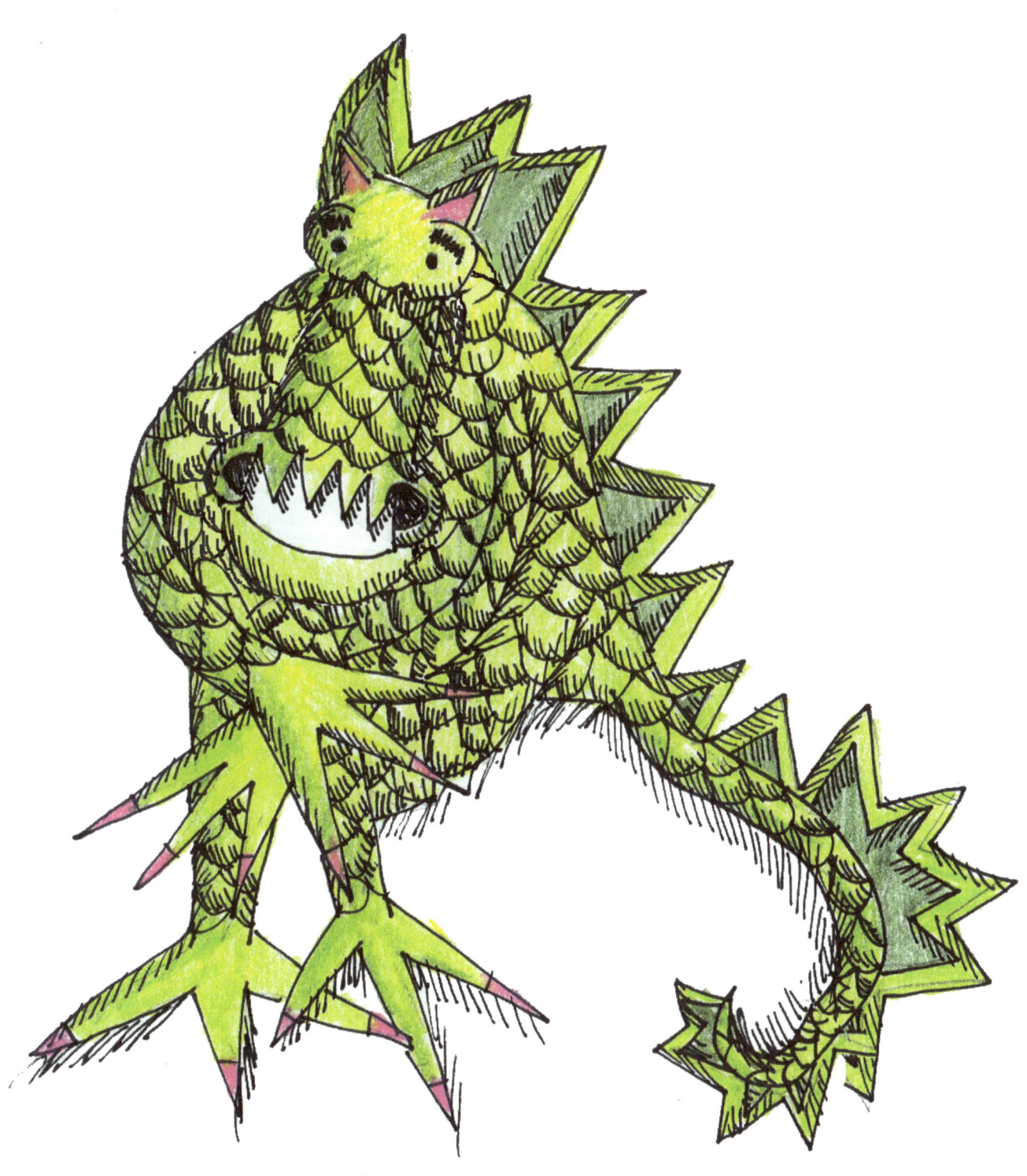

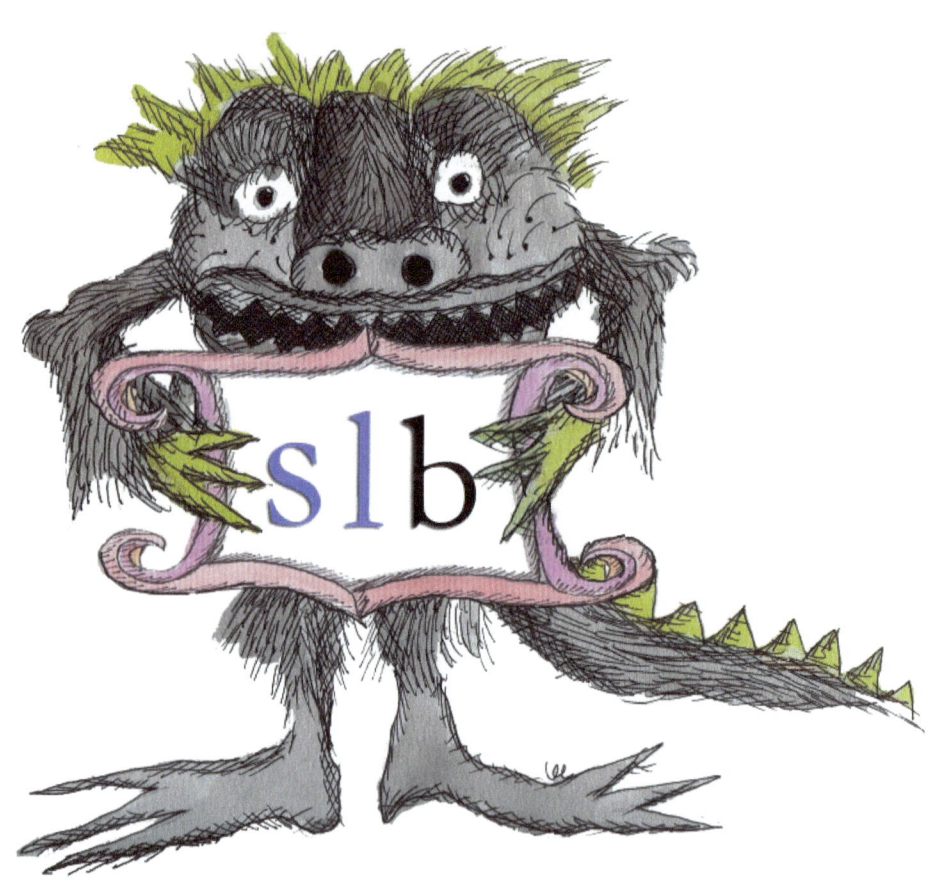

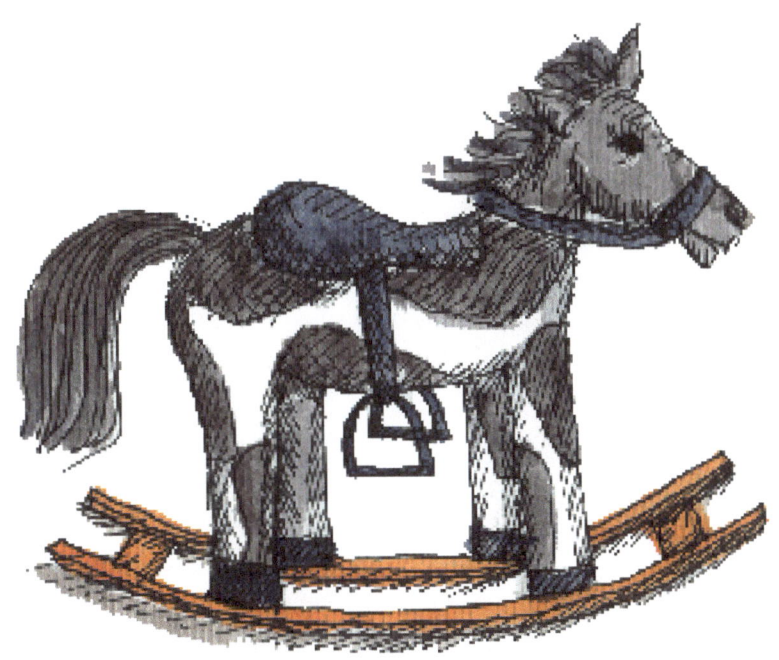

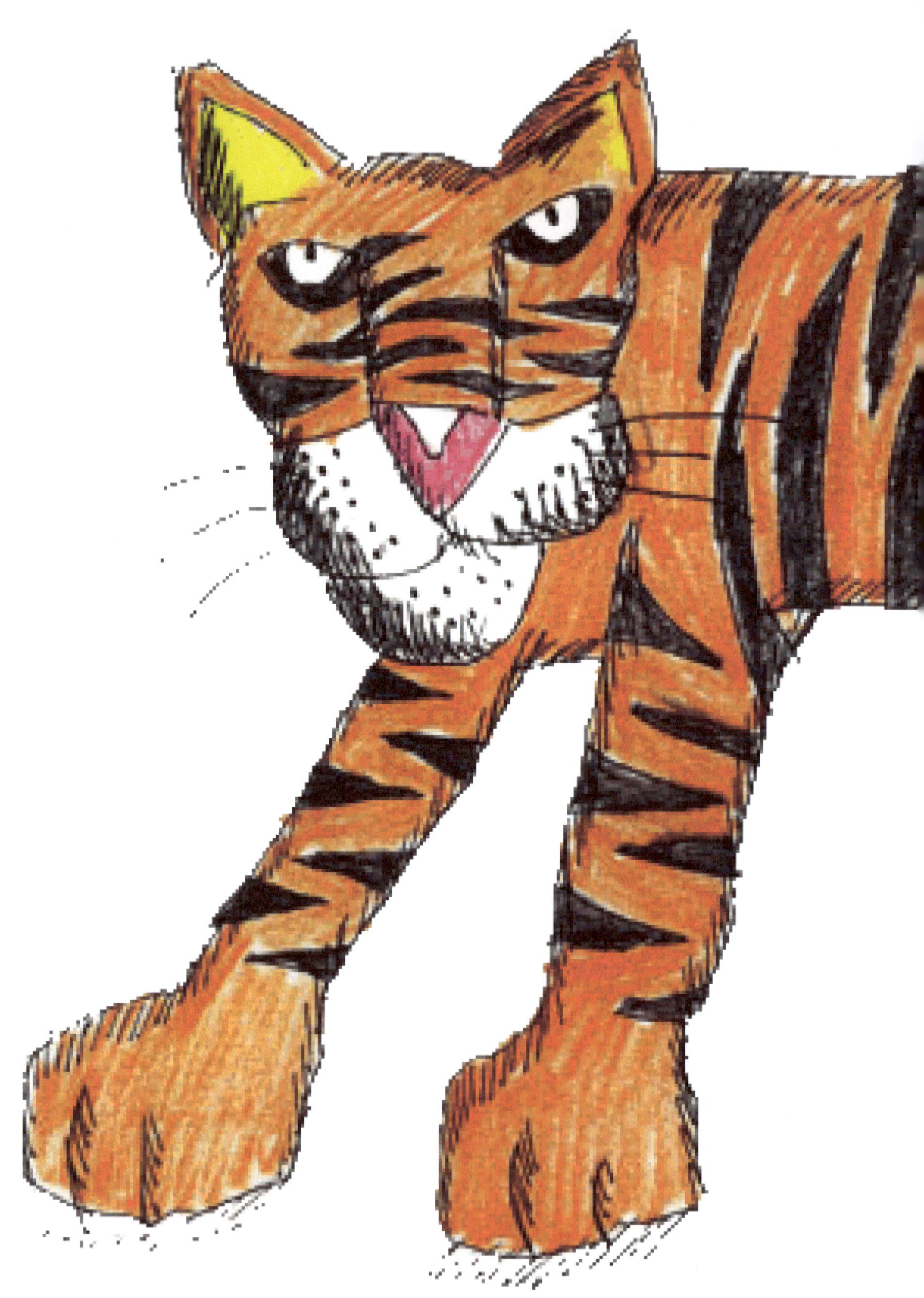

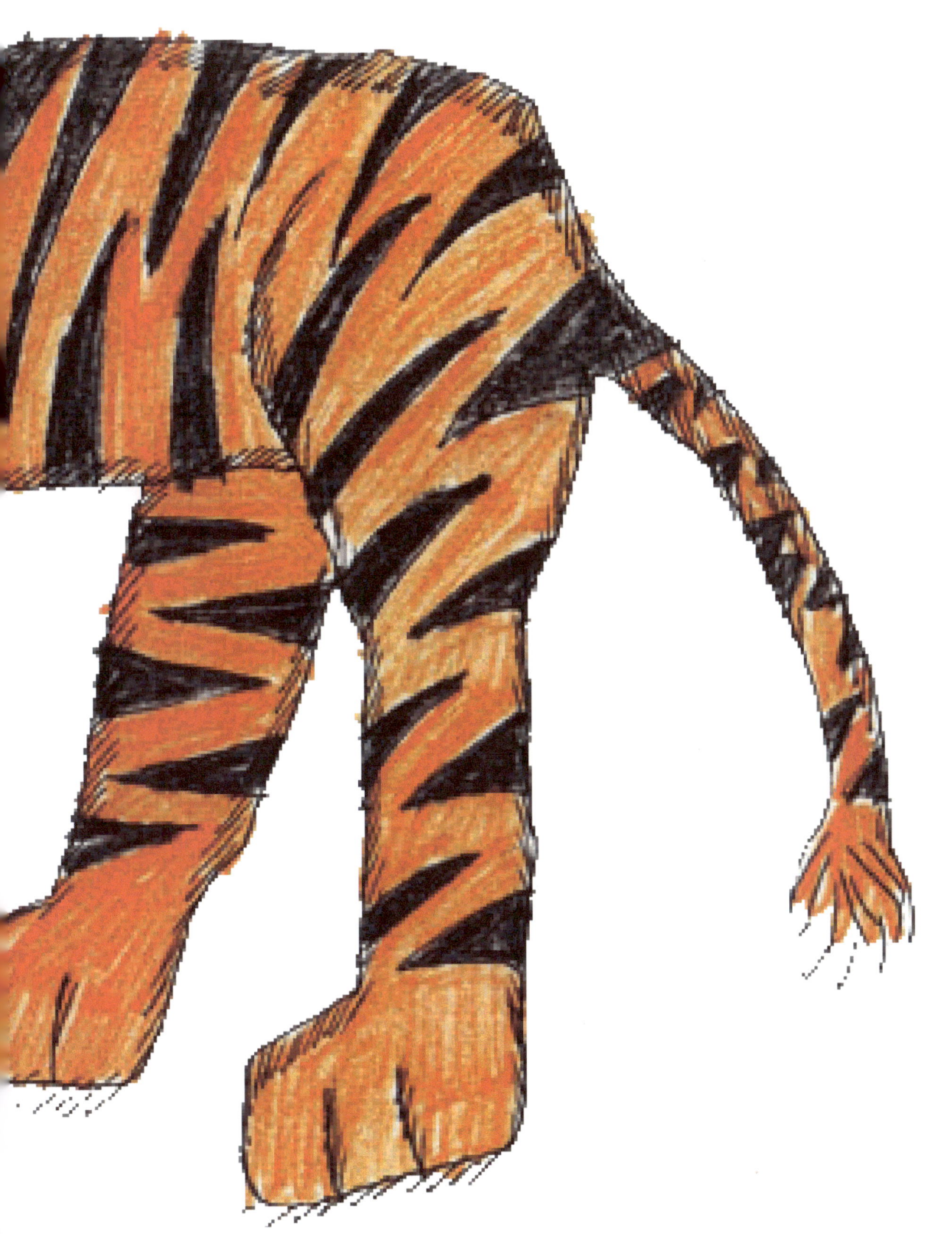

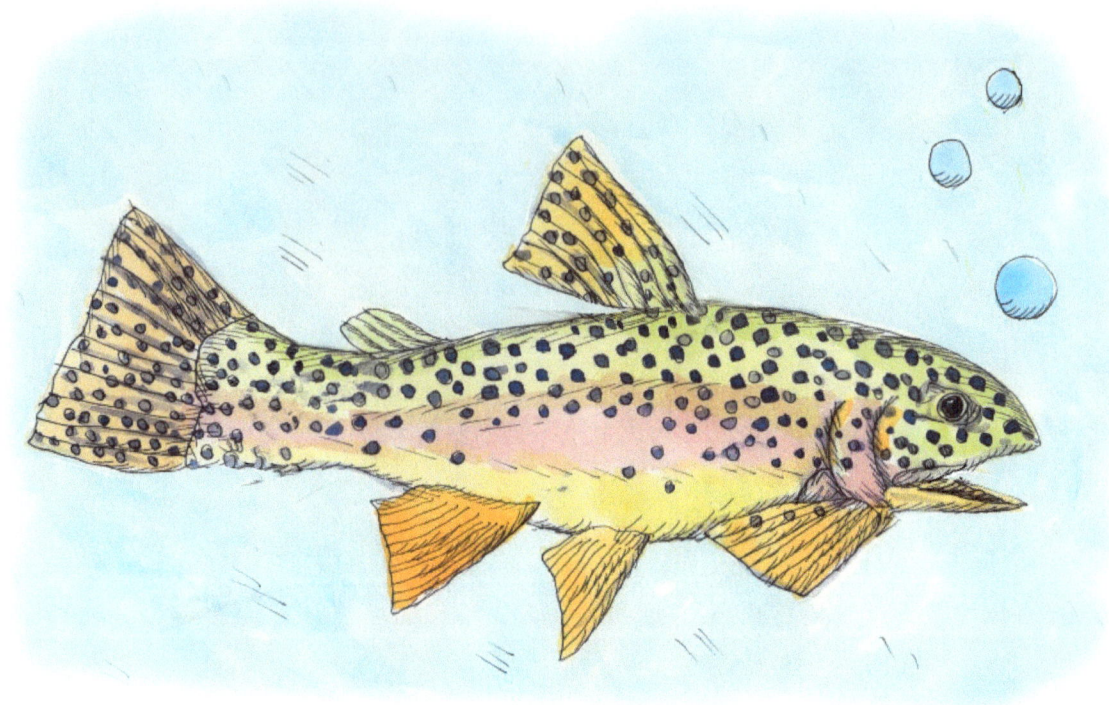

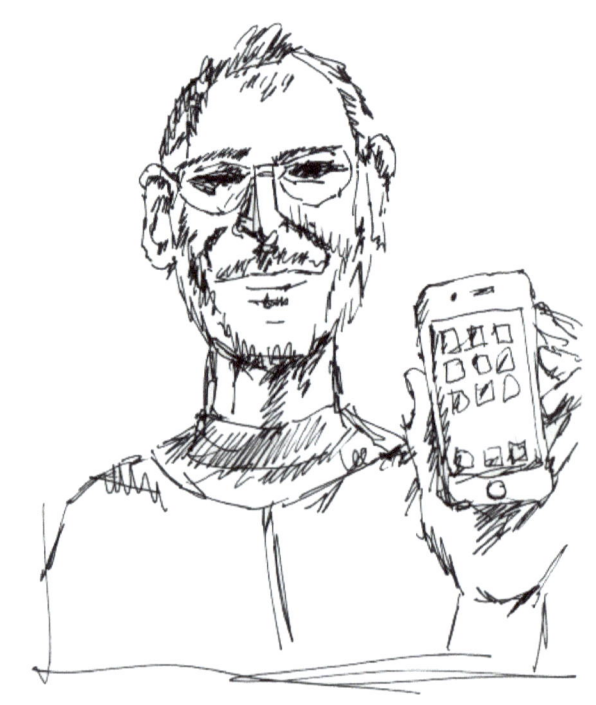

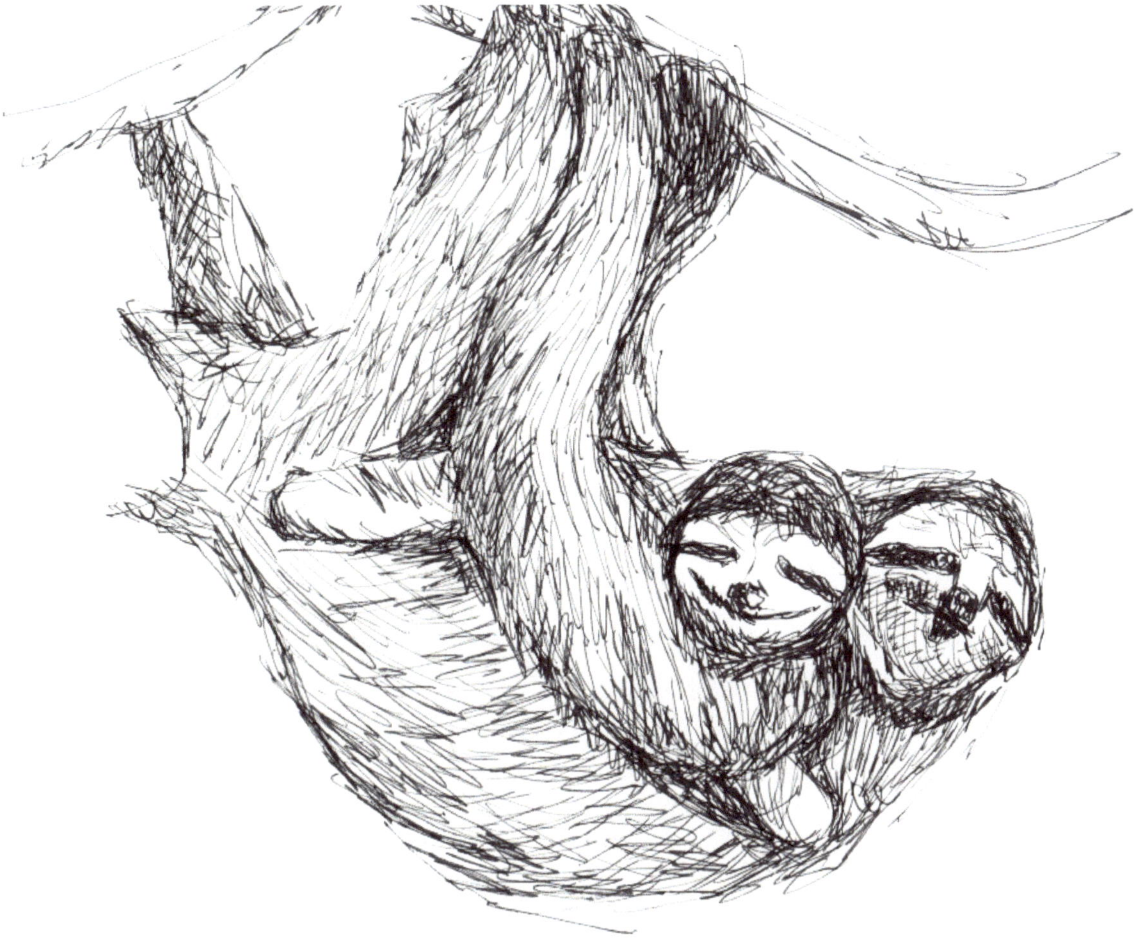

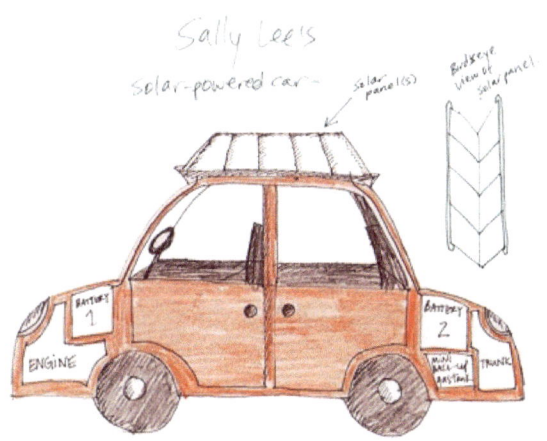

Sally Lee's

solar-powered car — solar panel(s)

Birdseye view of solar panel

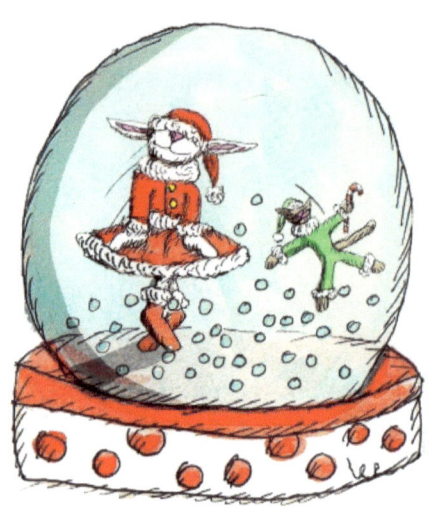

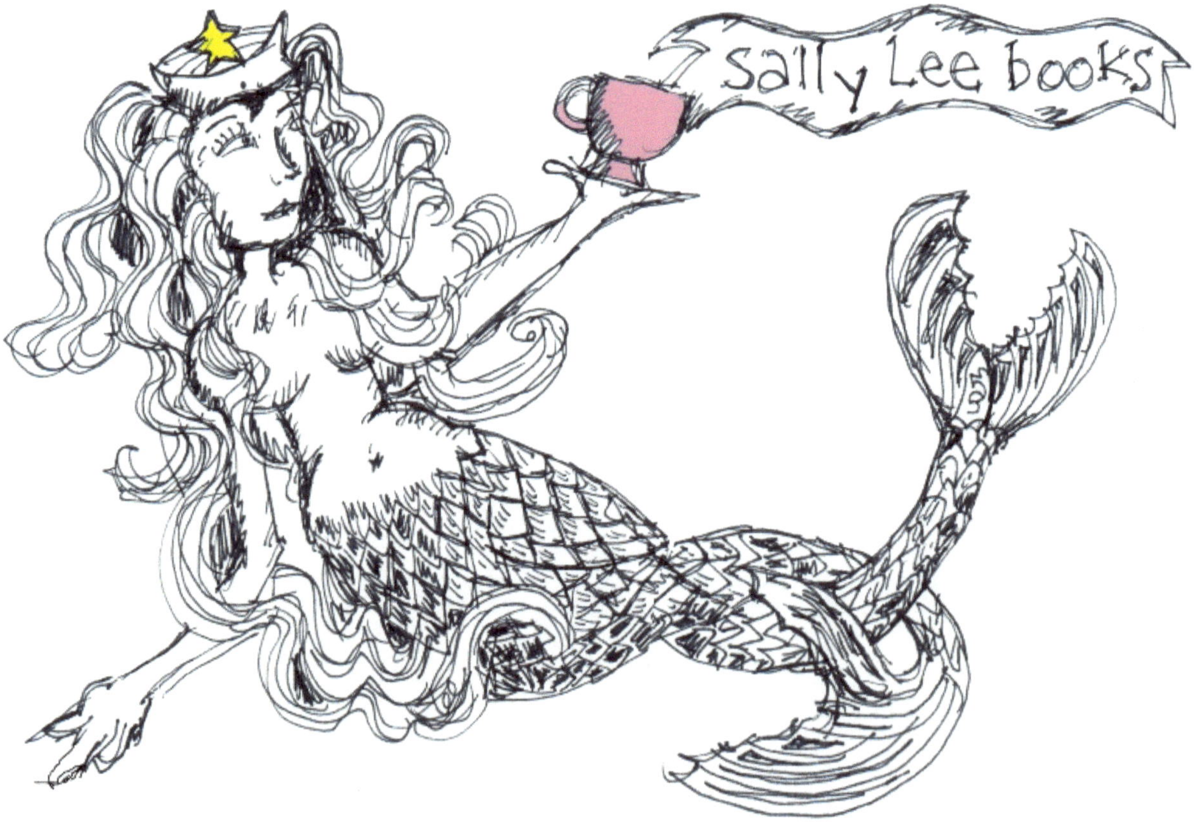

sally Lee books

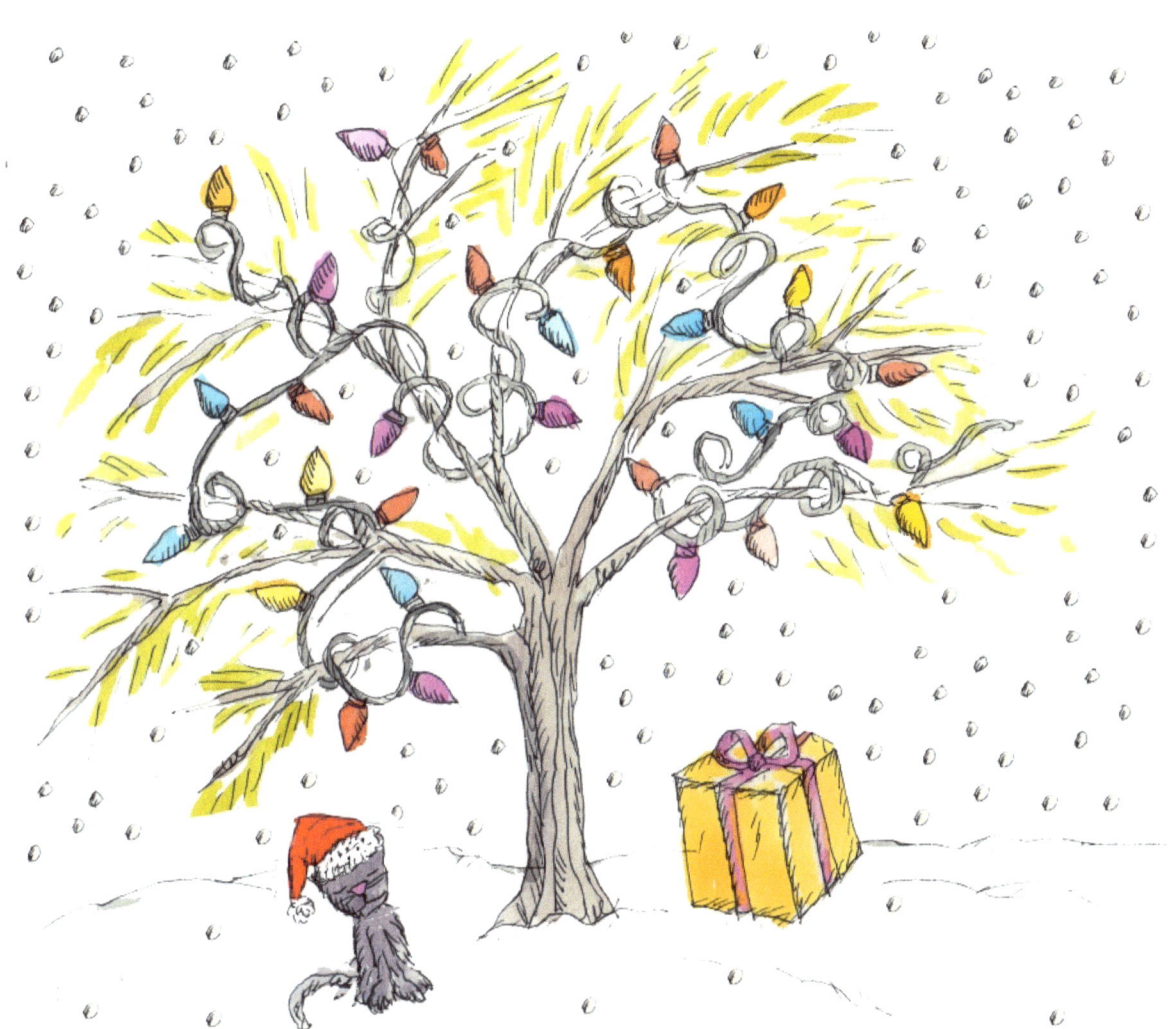

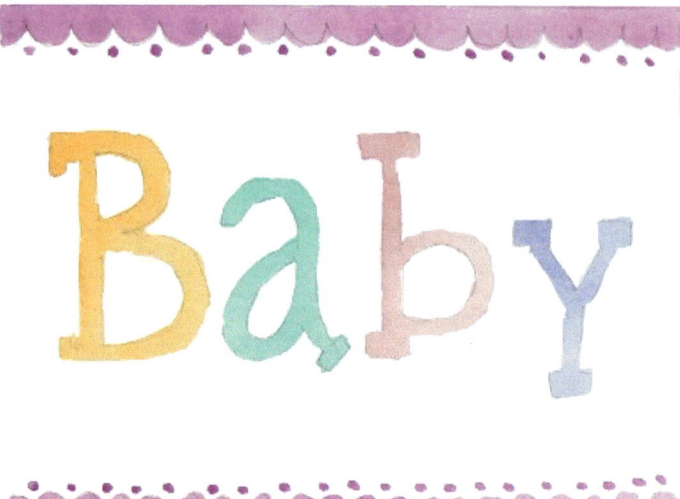

Baby

Sally Lee Books

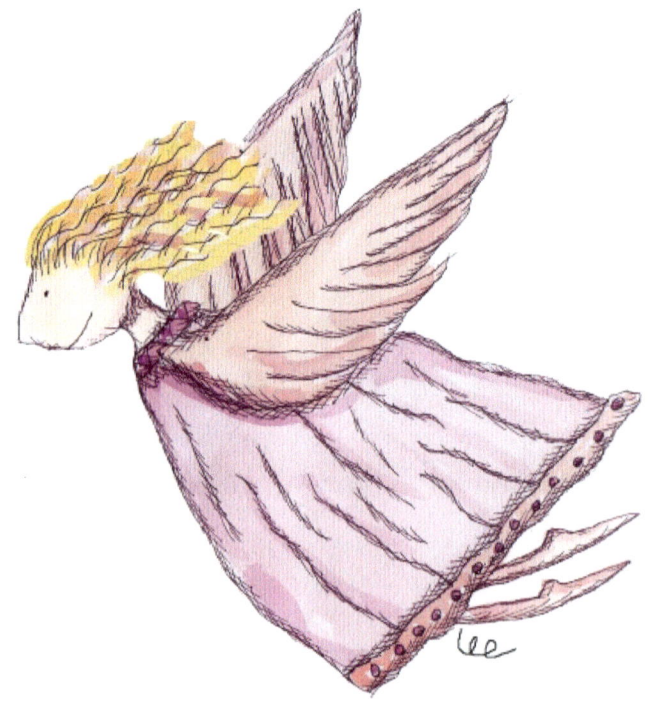

www.leepublishing.net

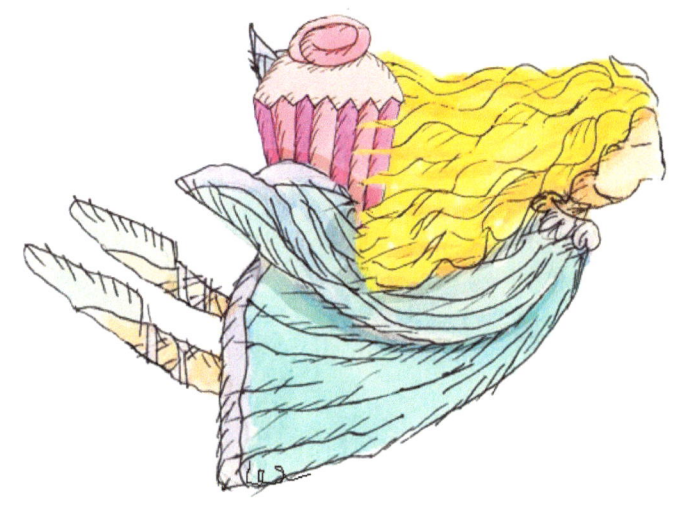

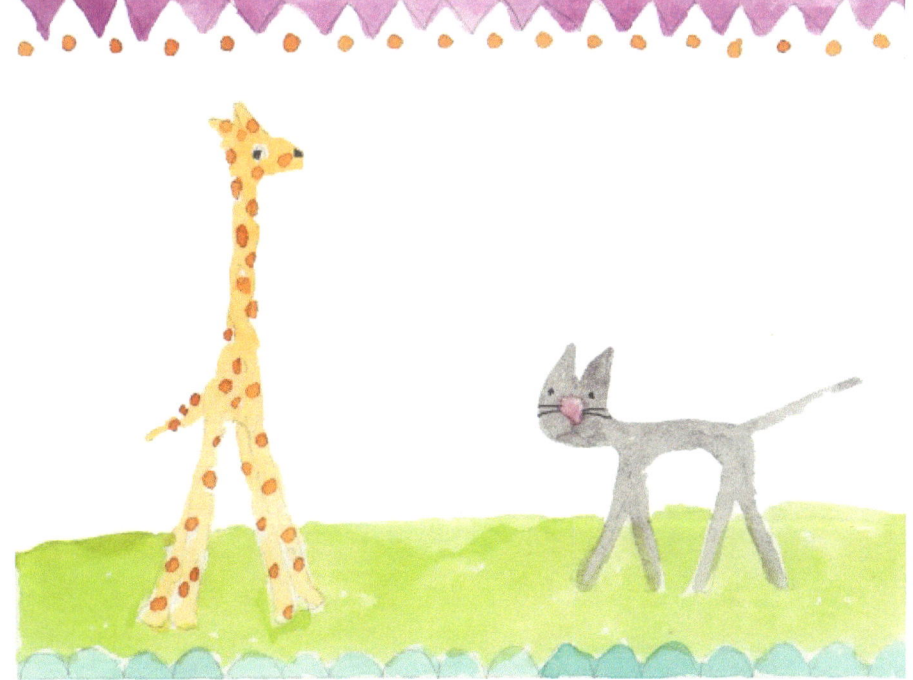

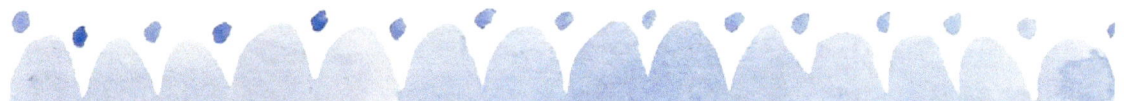

BABY

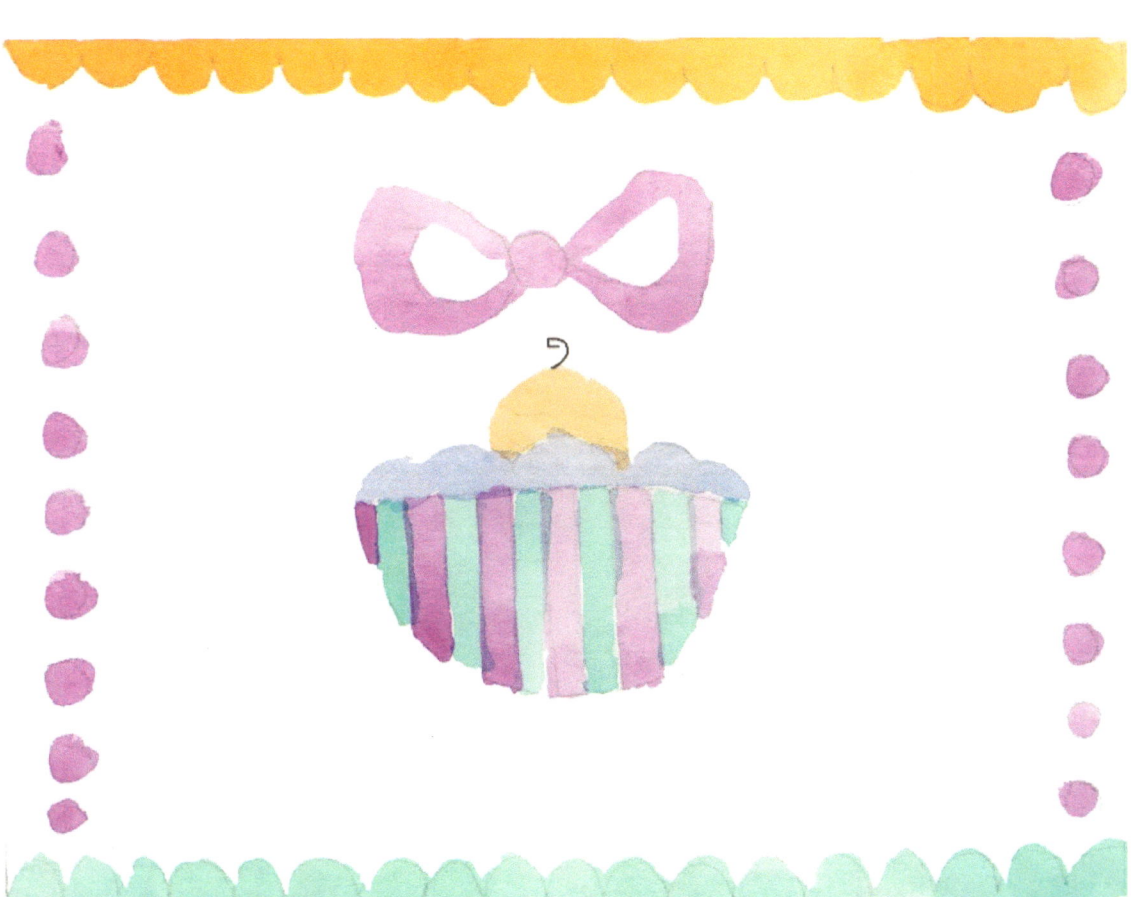

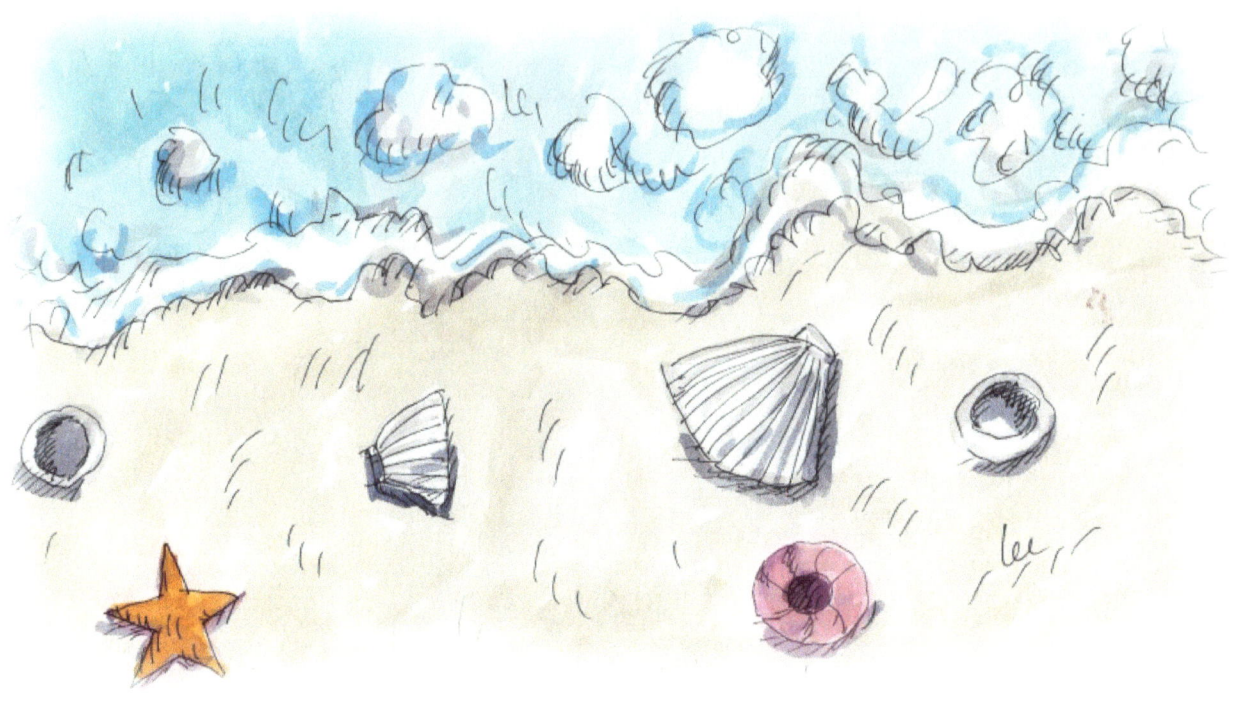

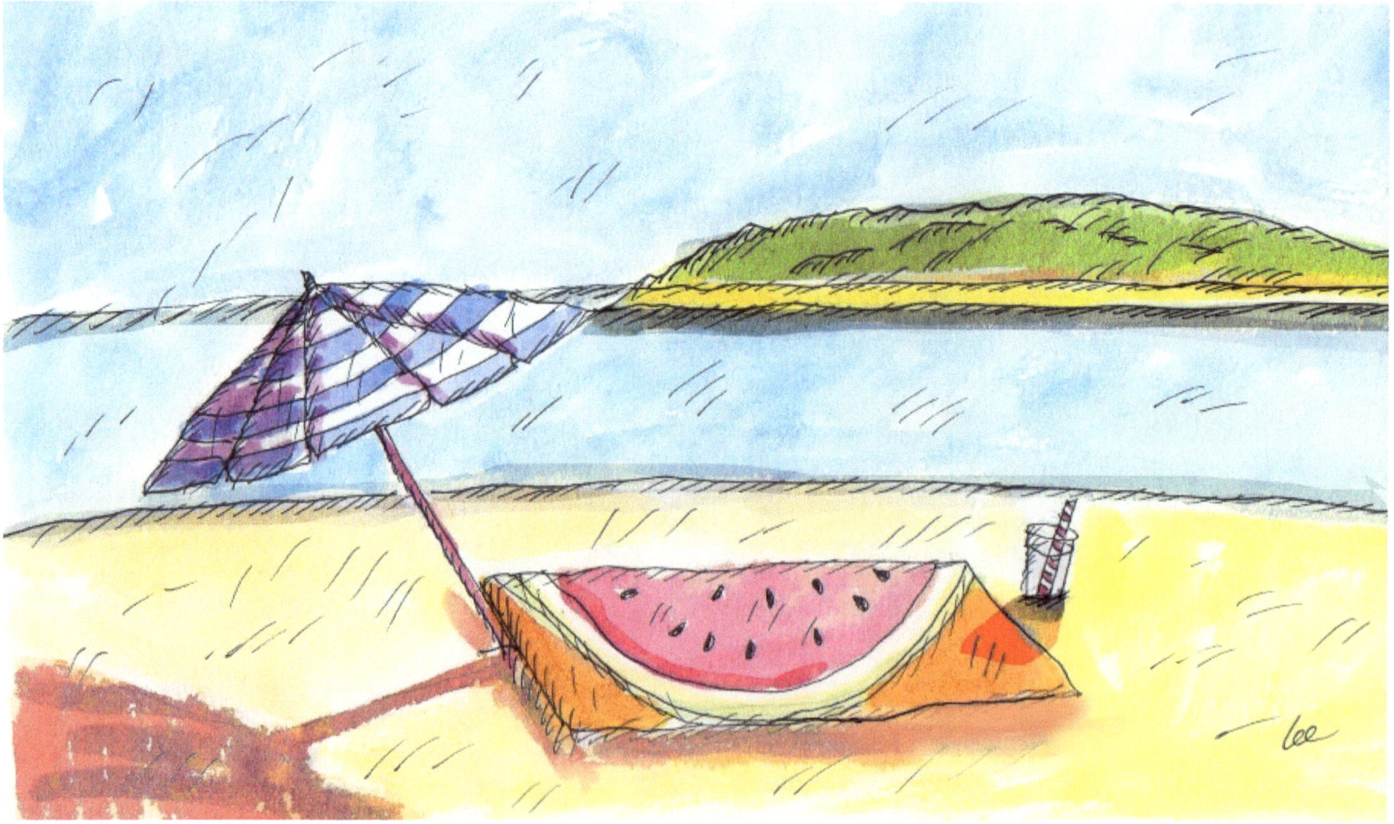

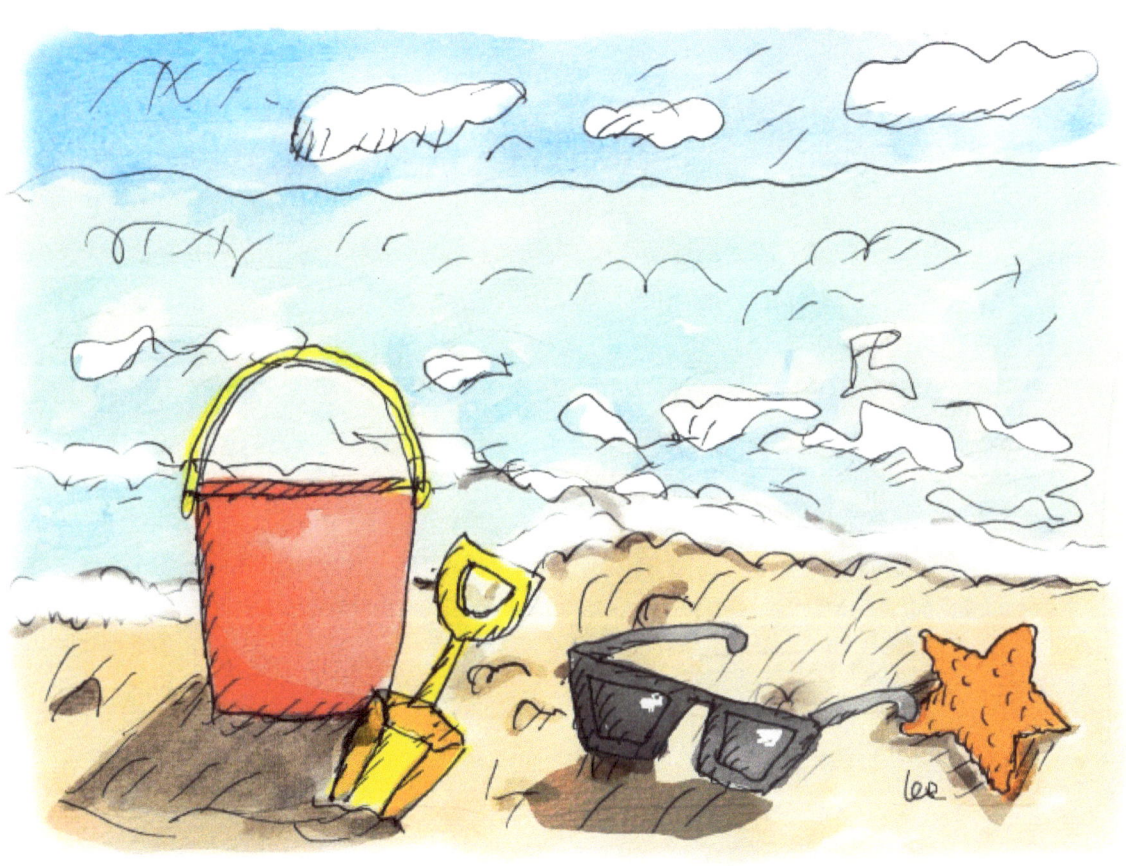

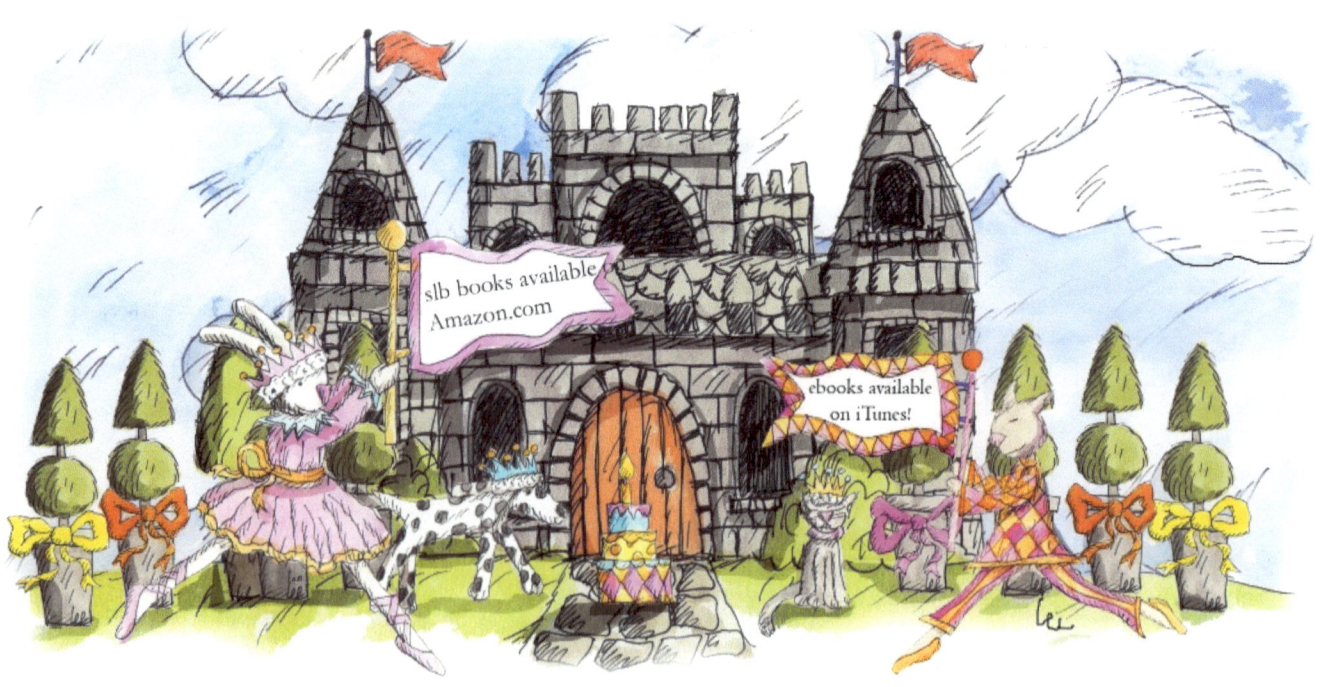

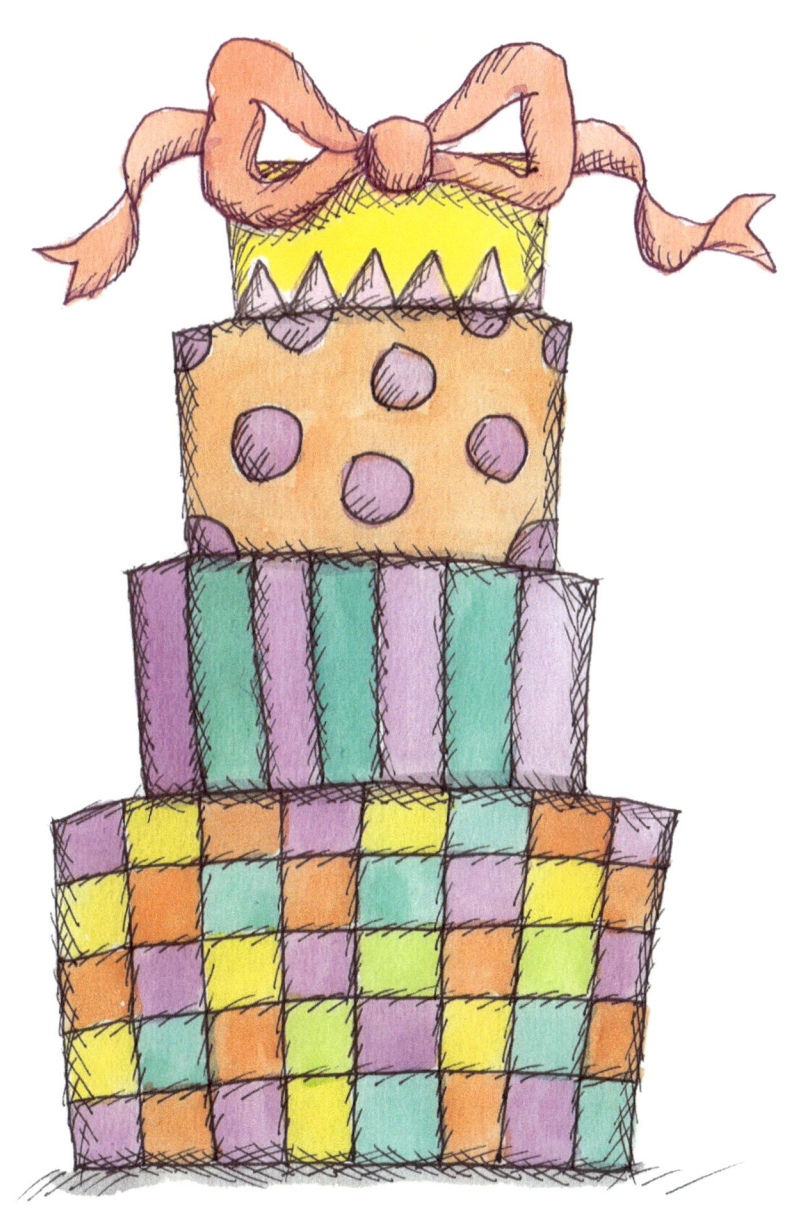

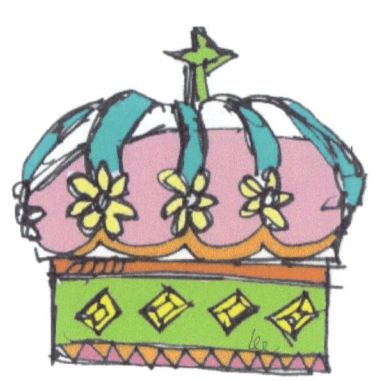
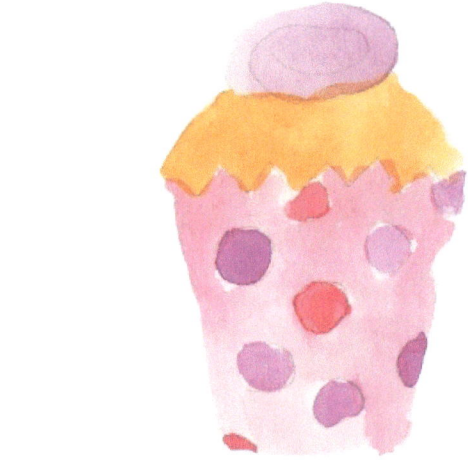
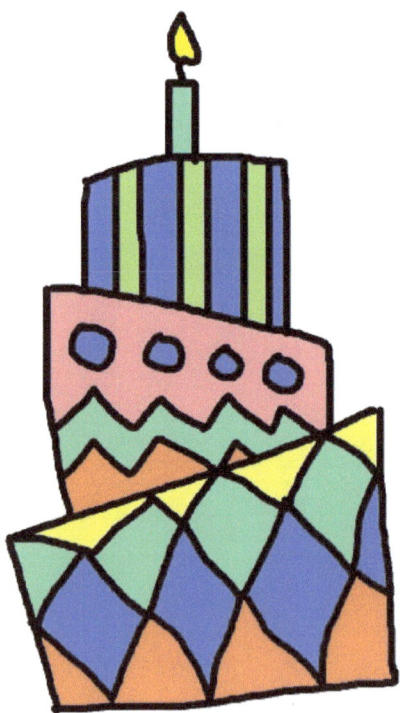
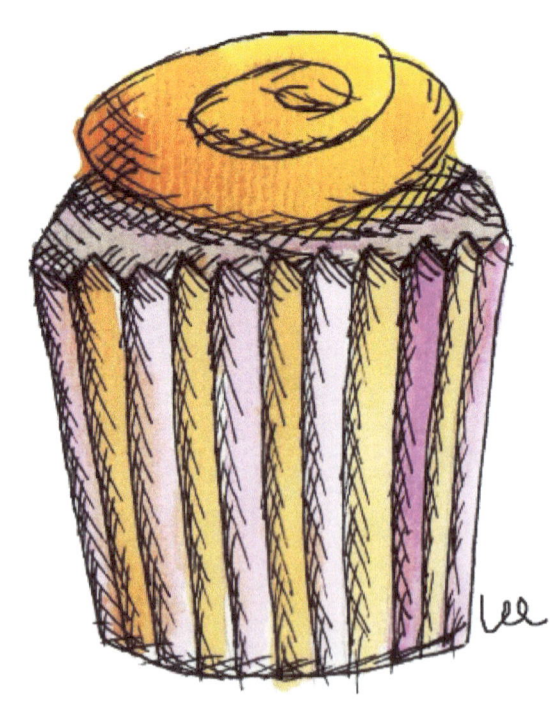

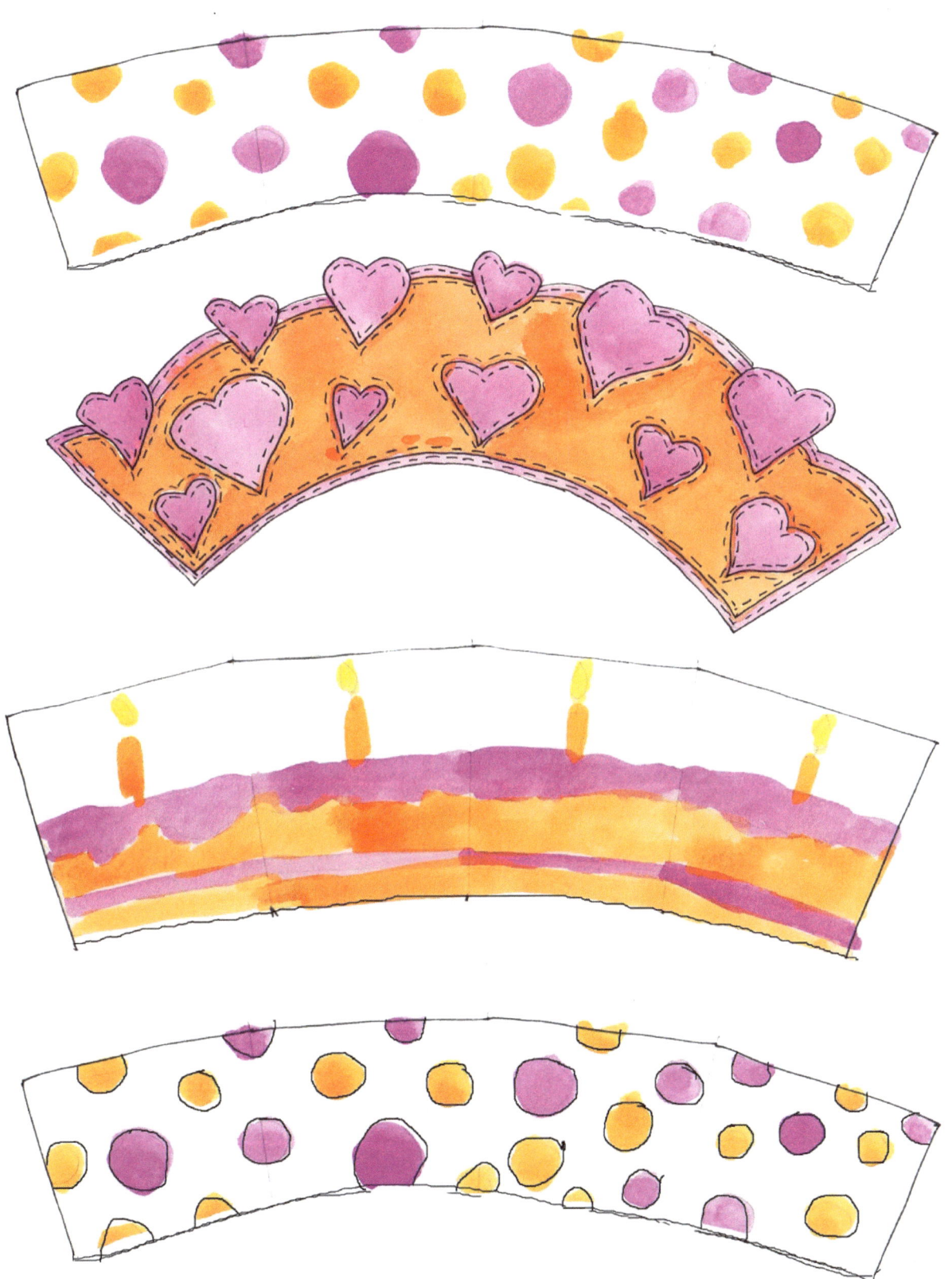

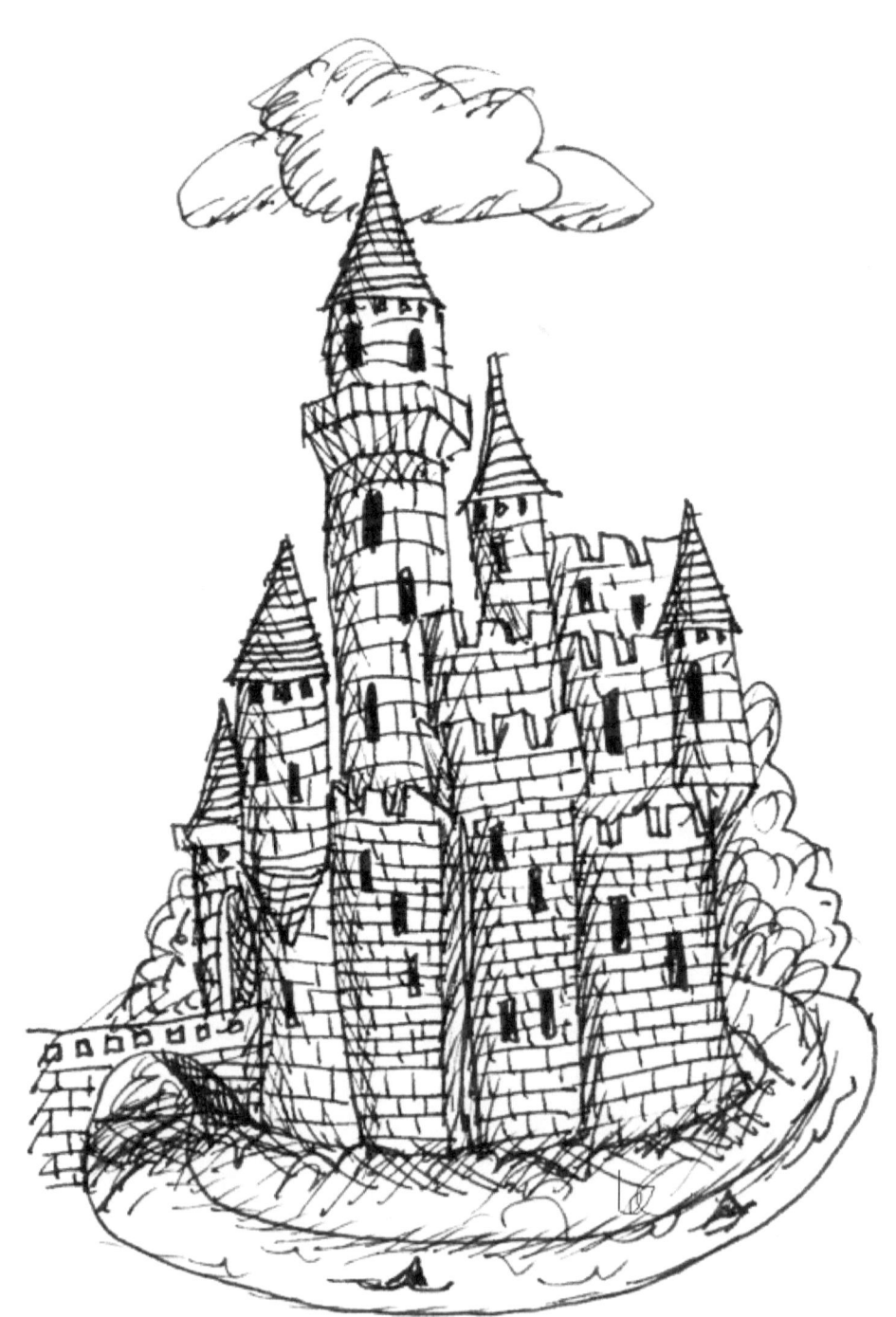

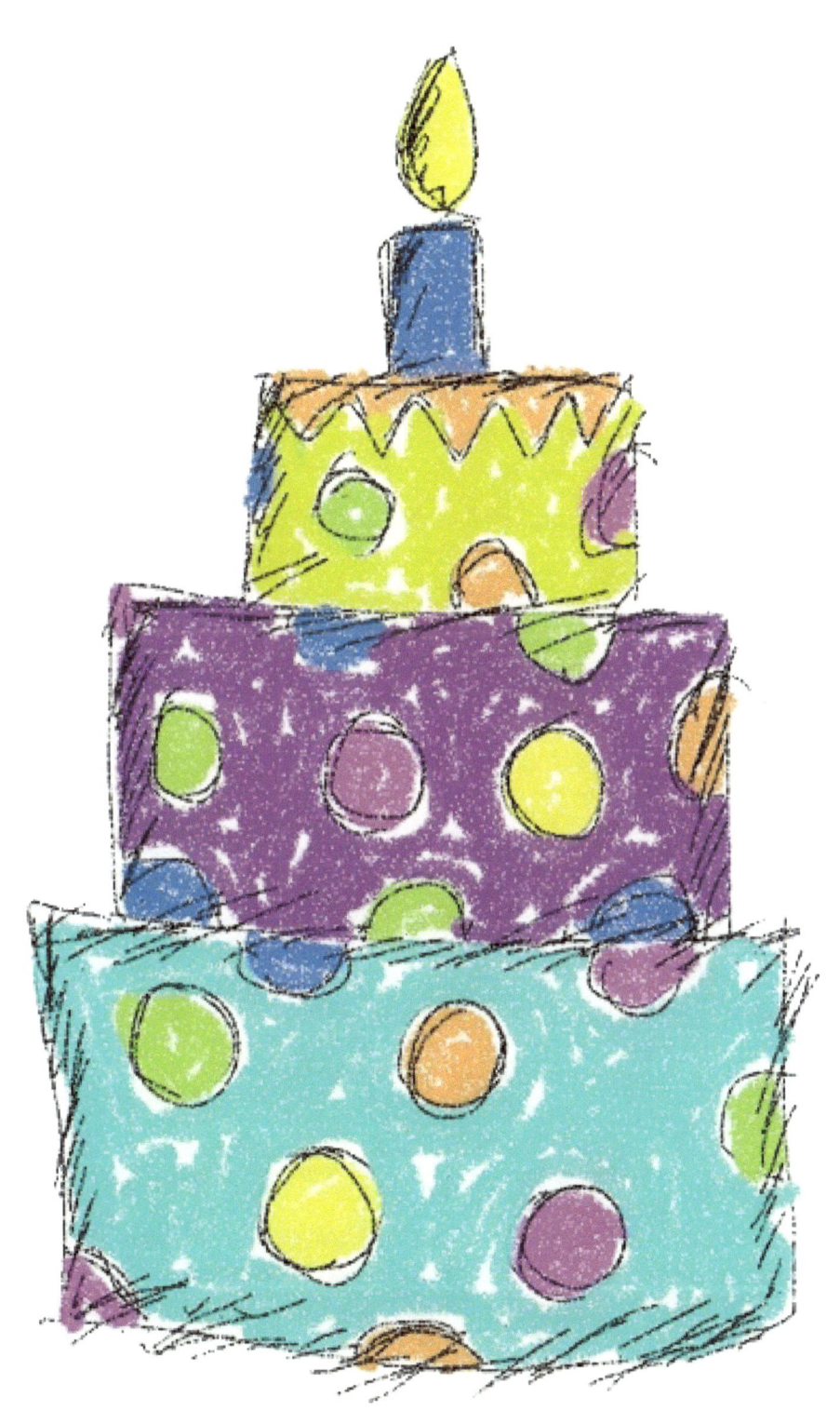

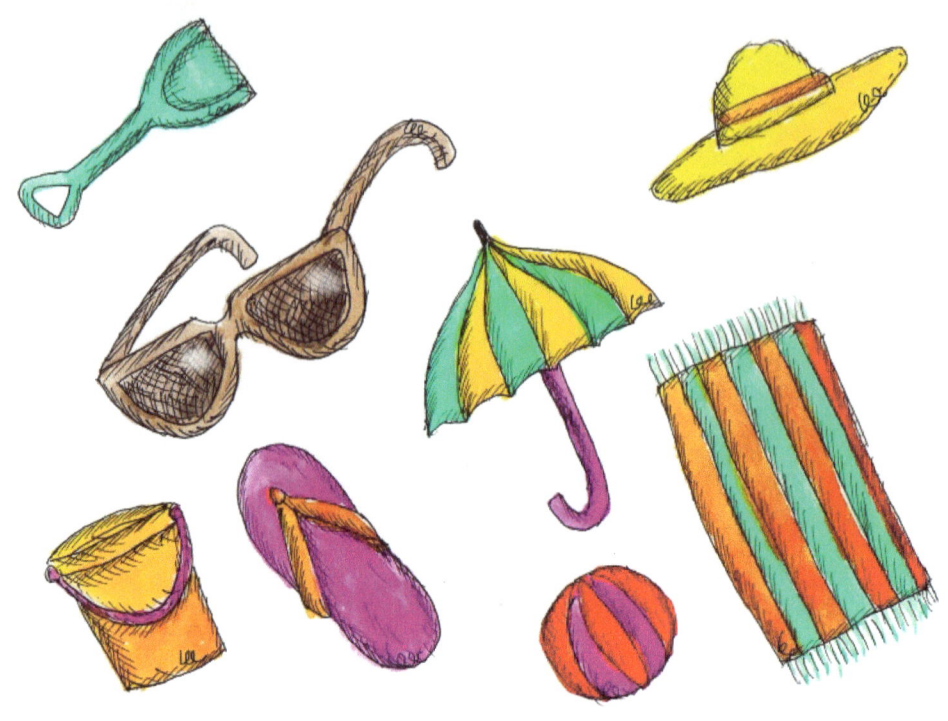
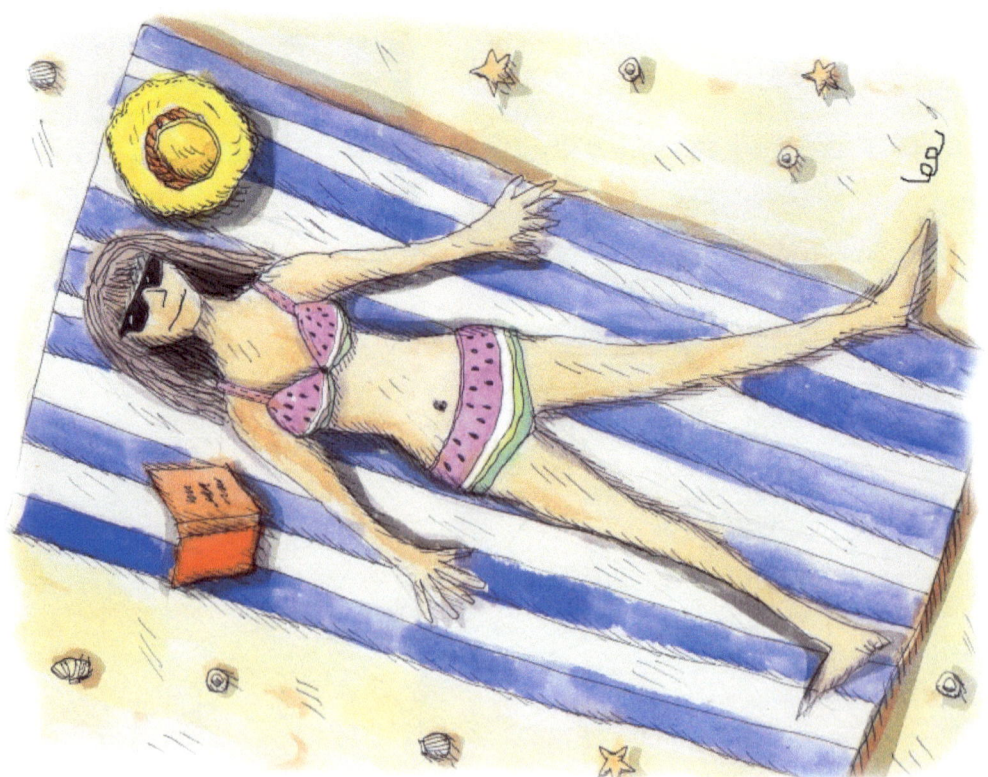

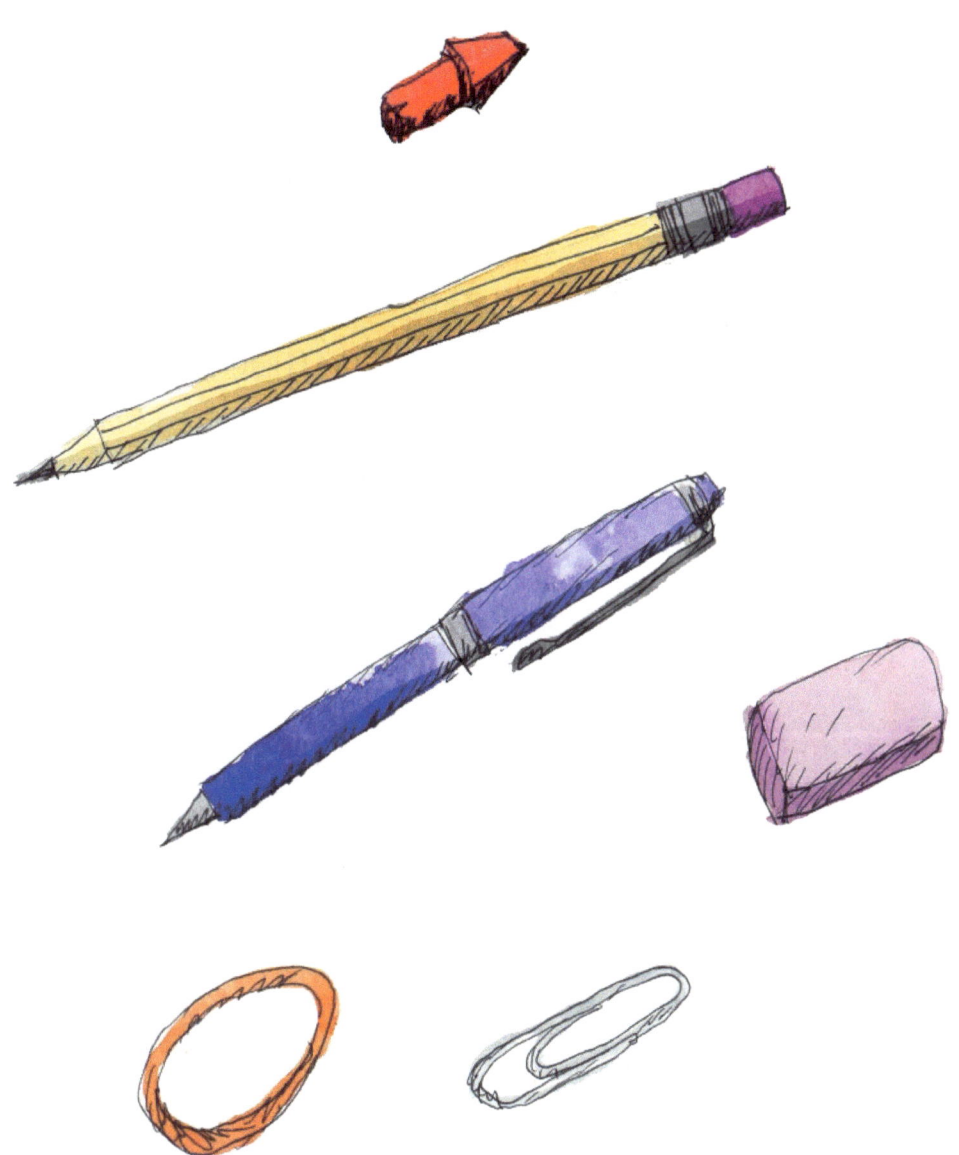

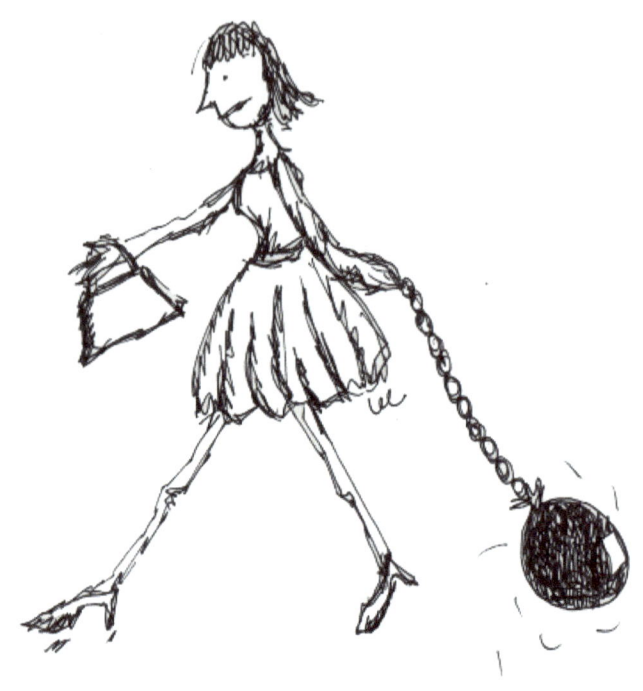

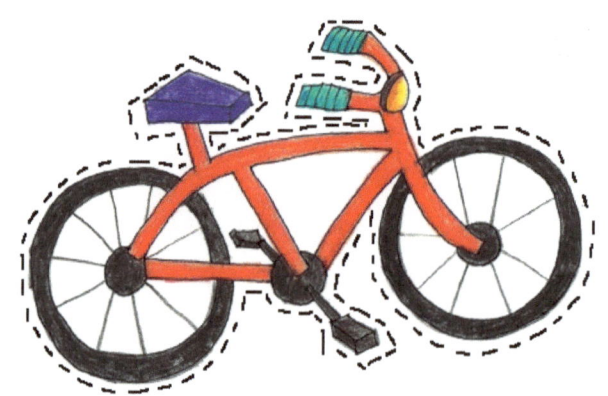

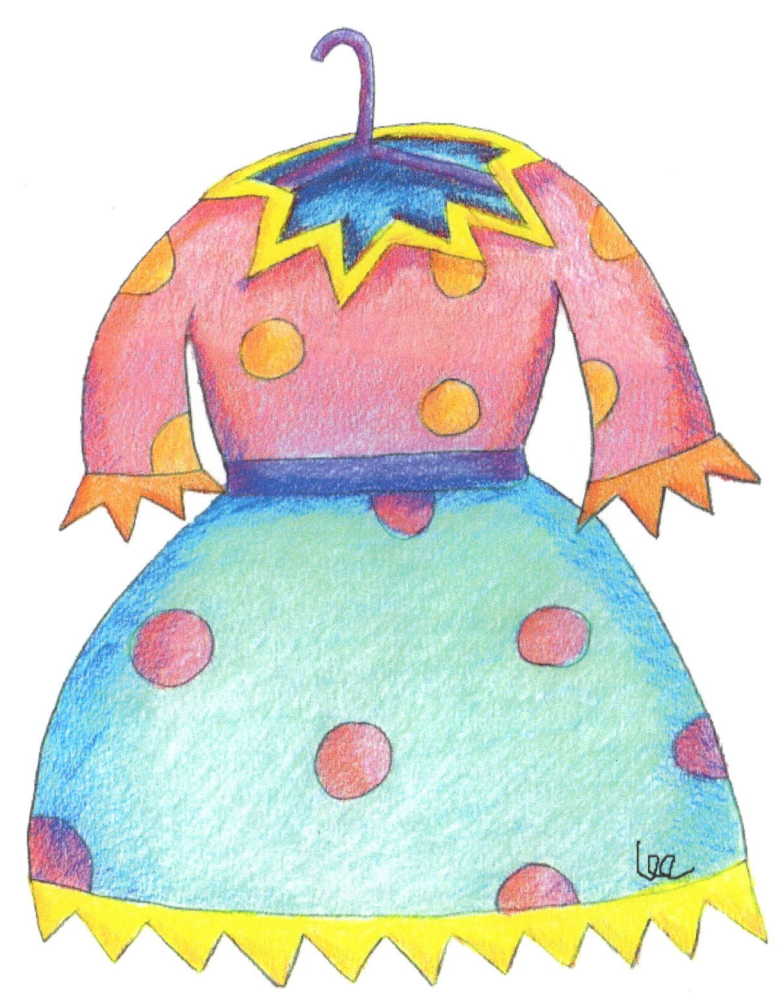

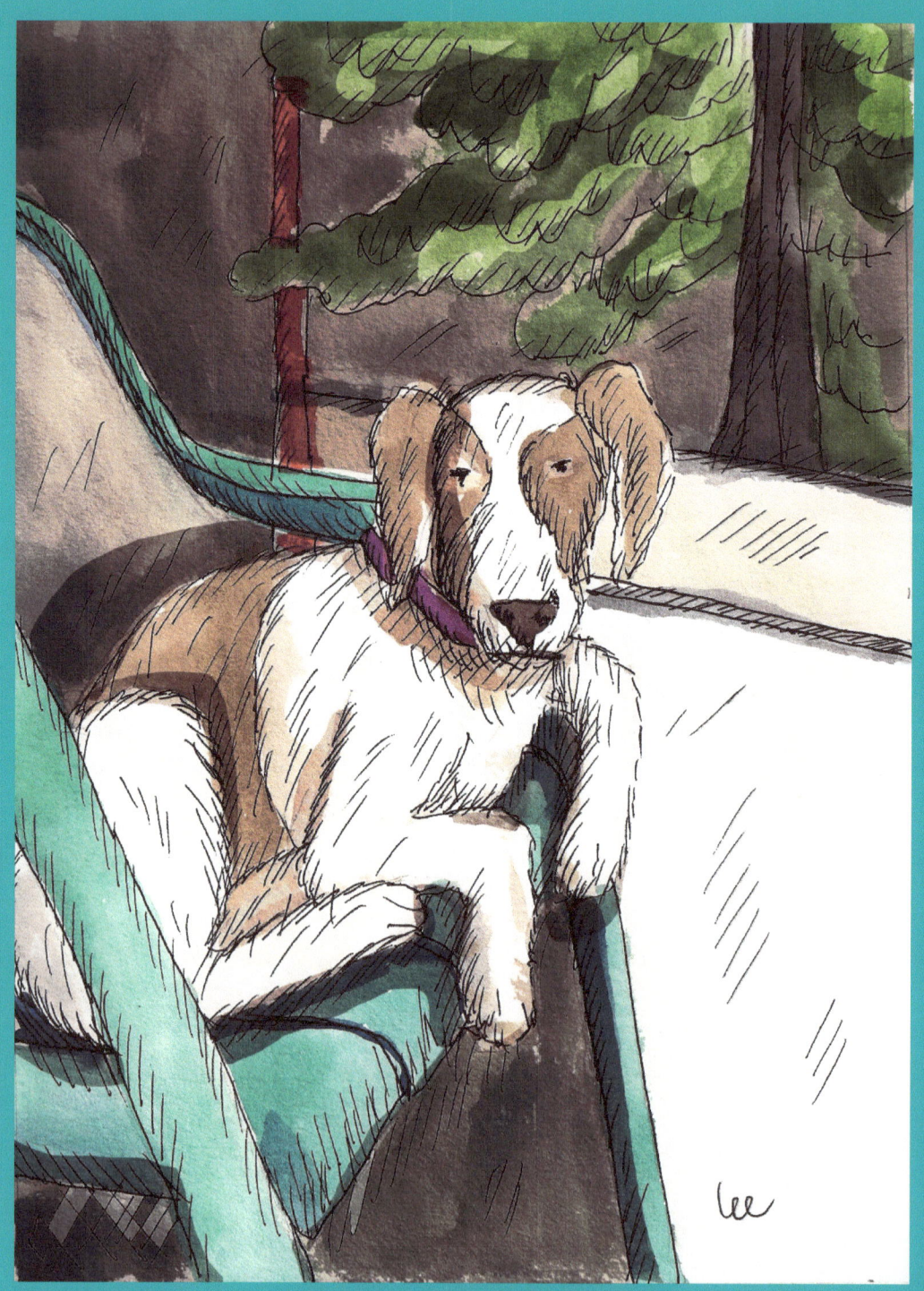

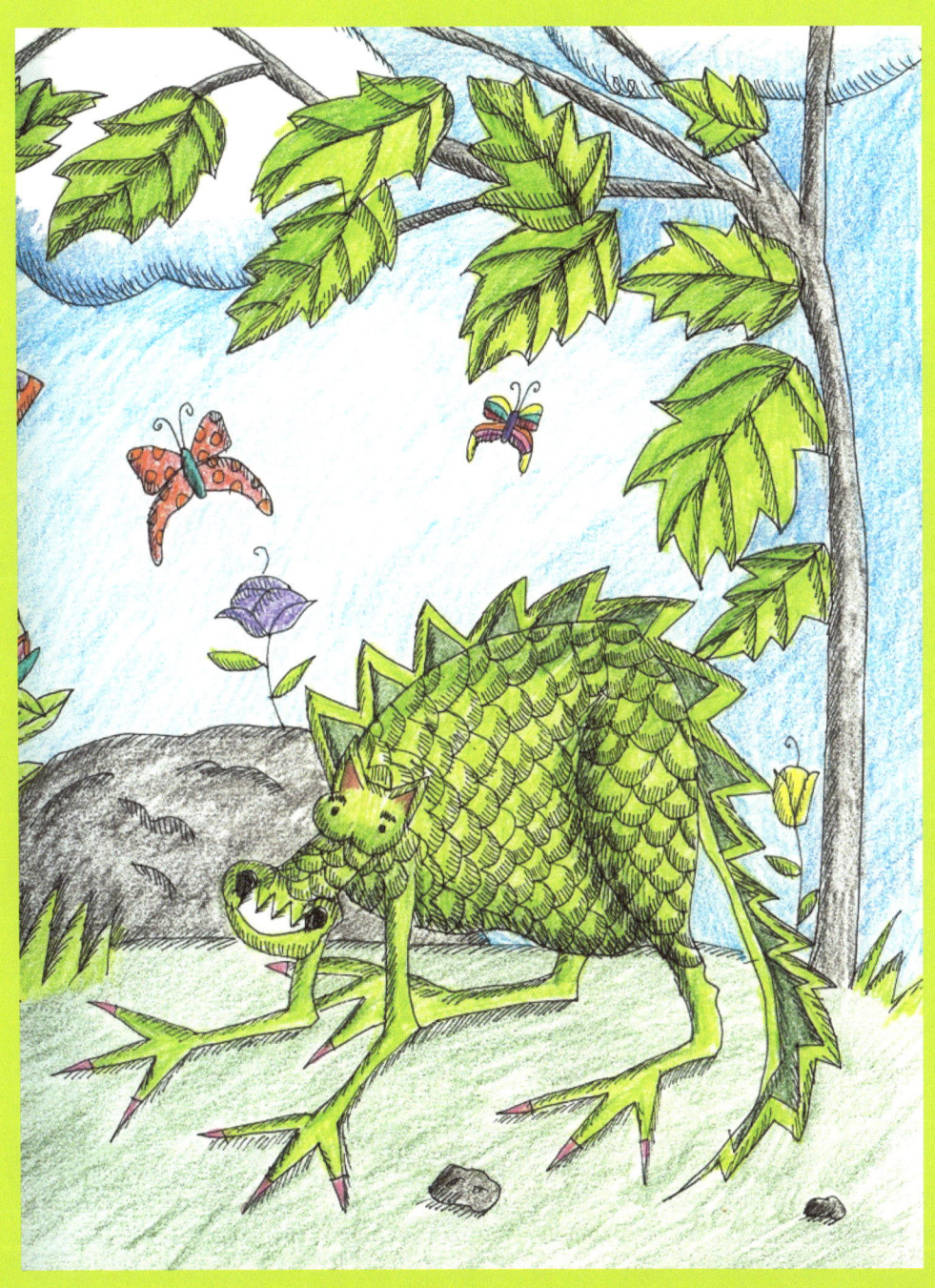

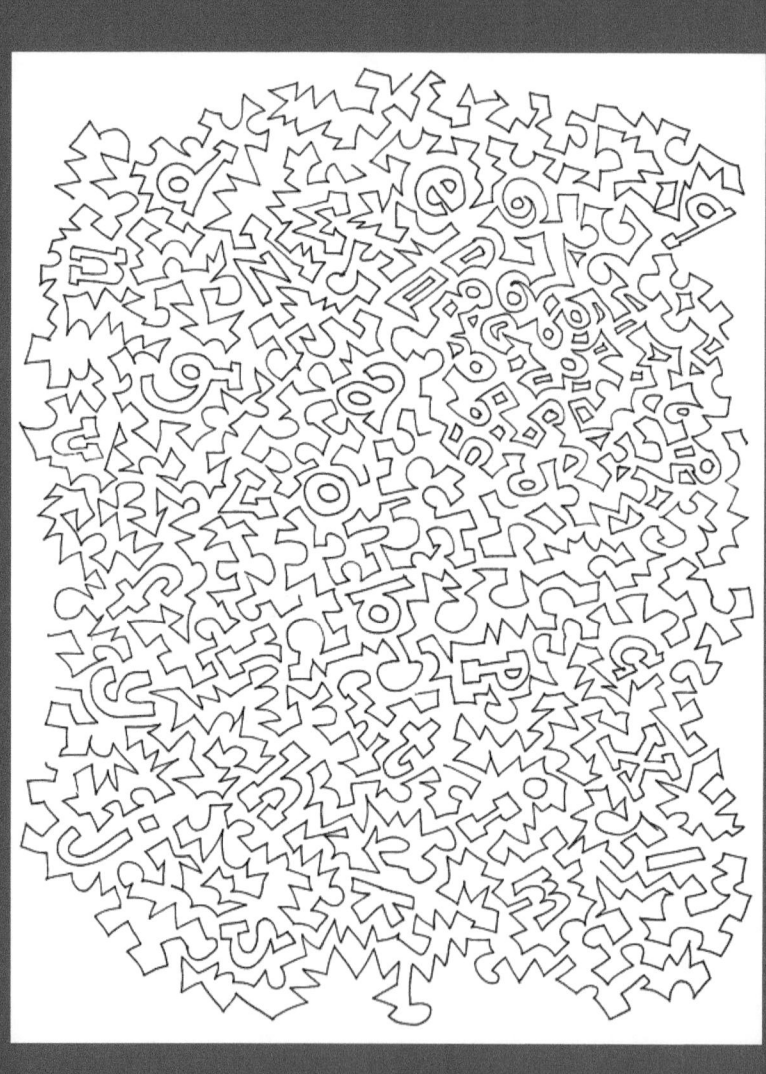

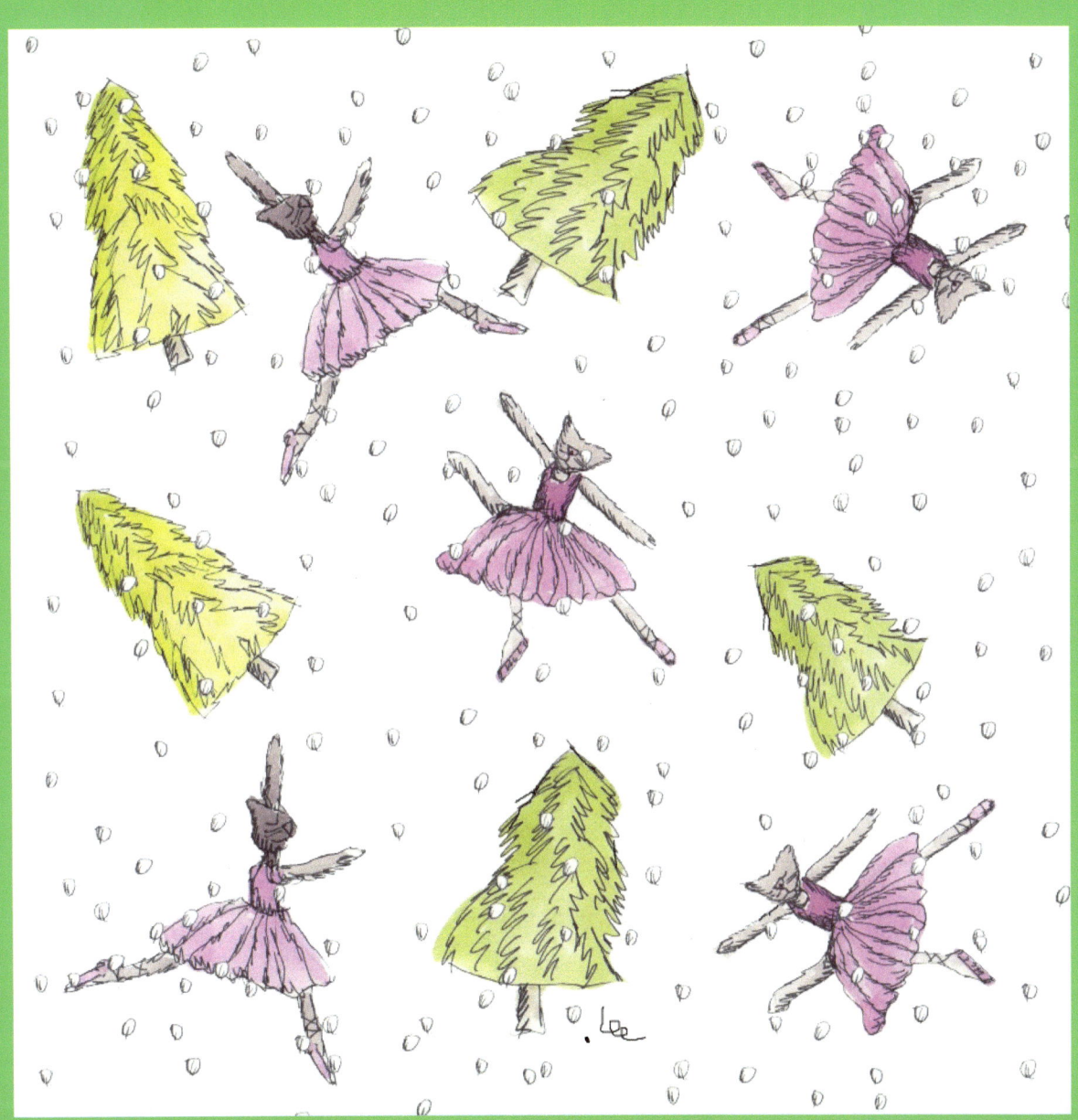

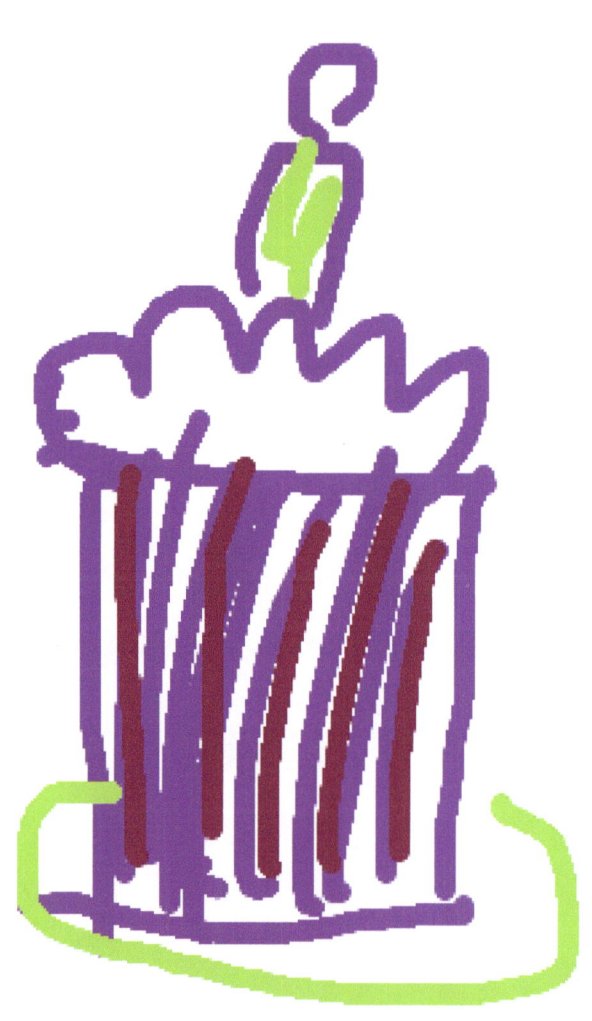

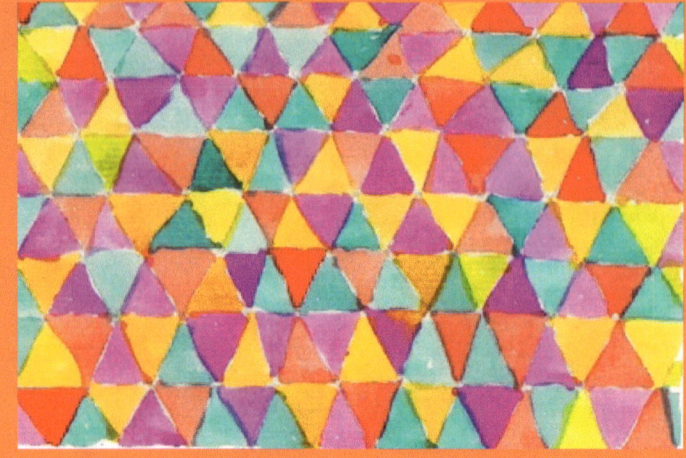

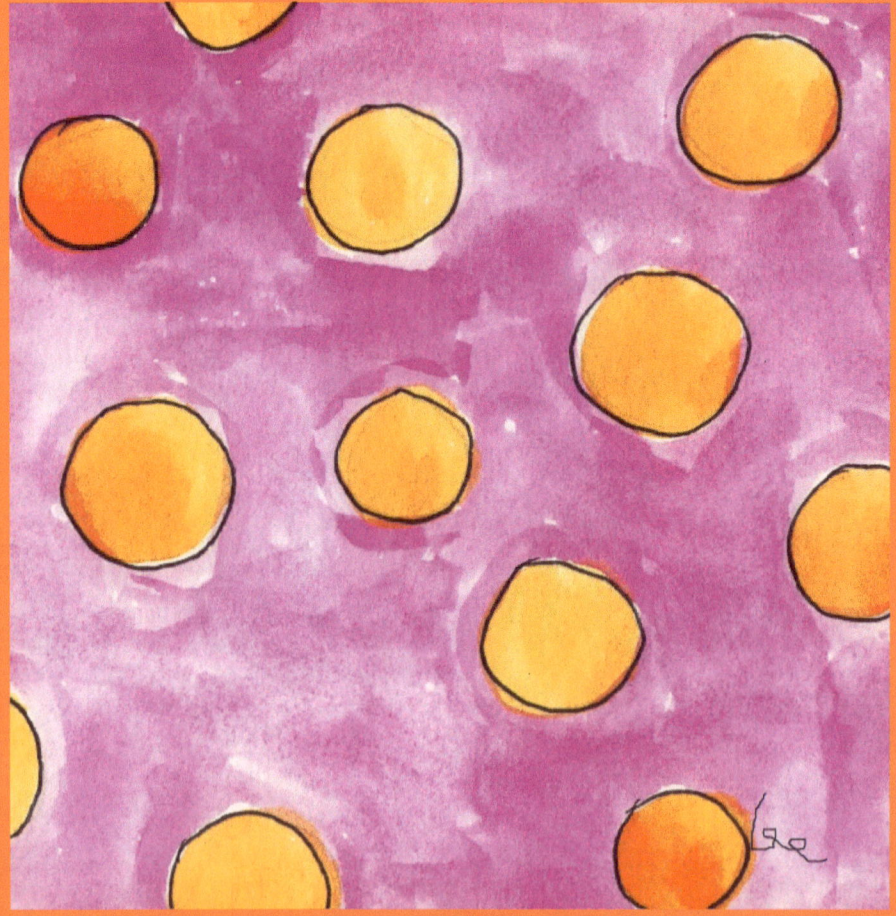

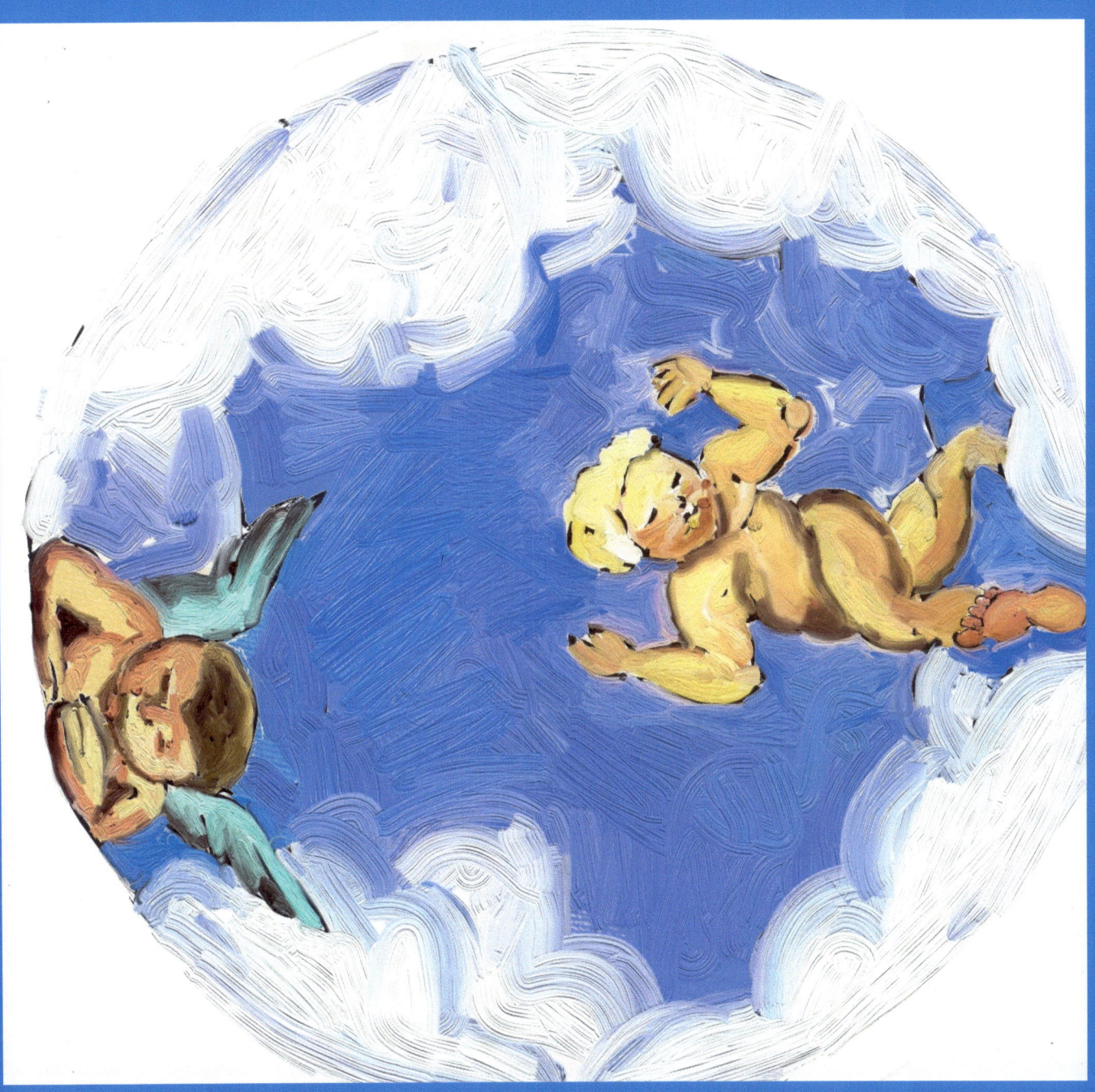

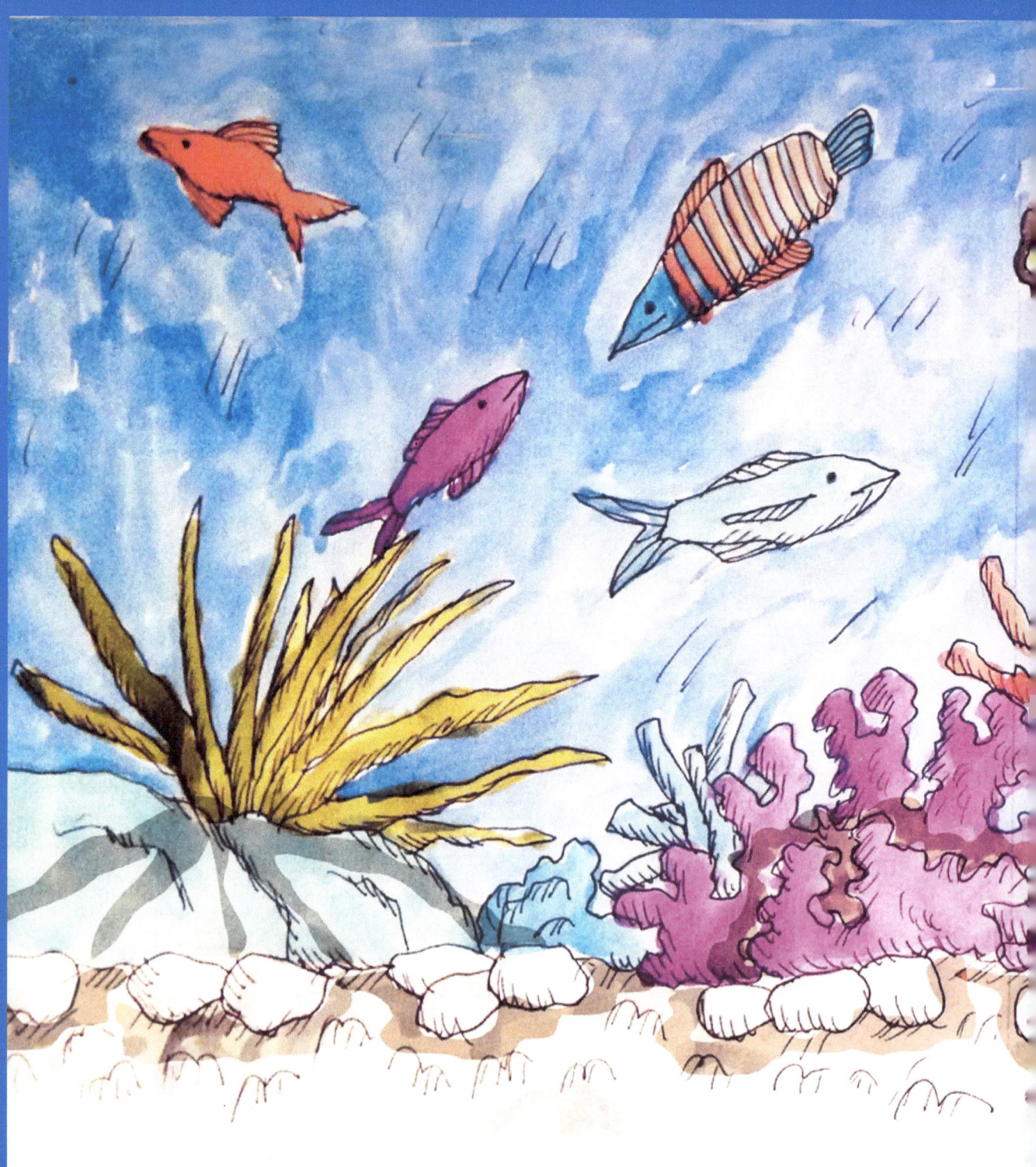

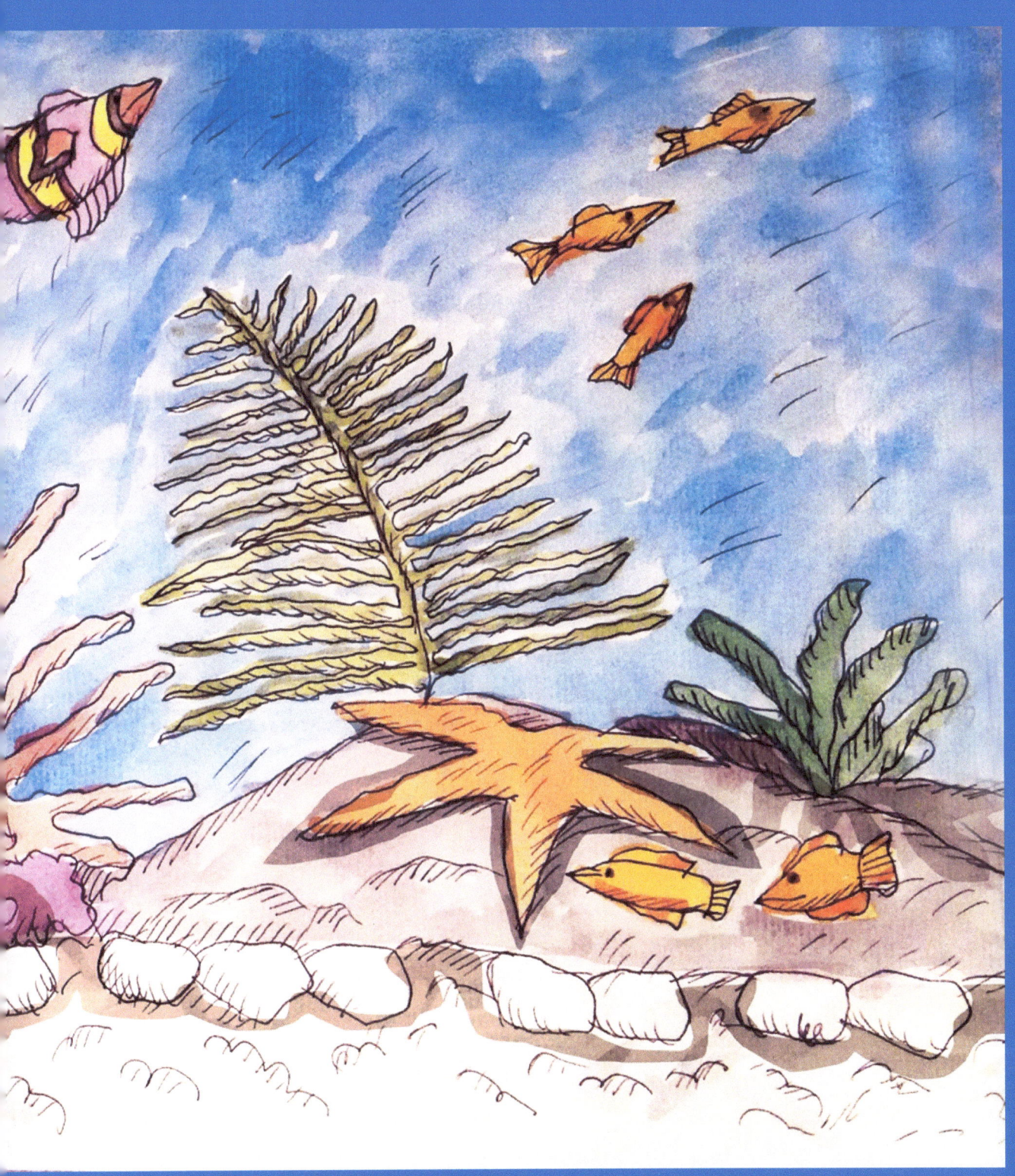

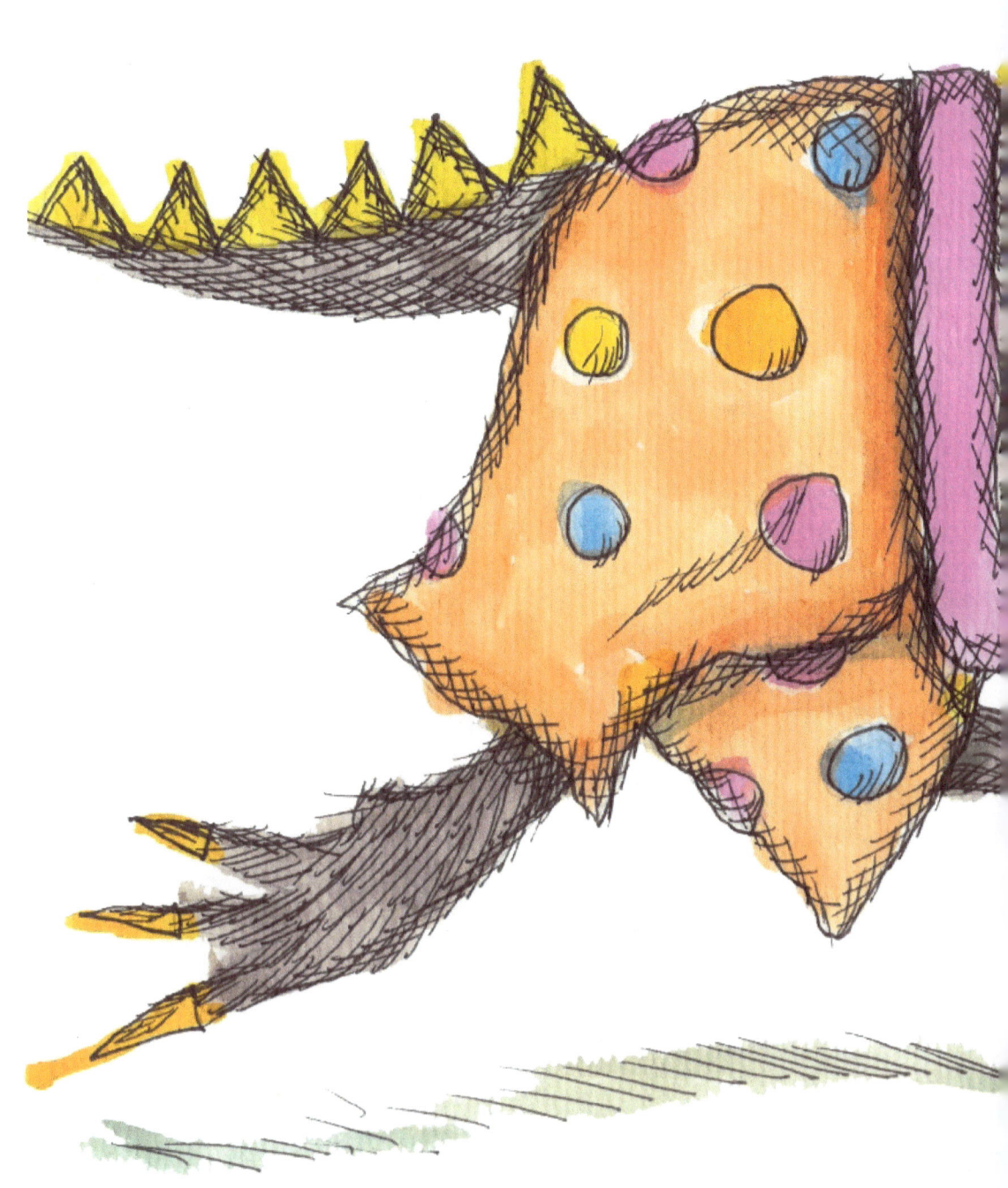

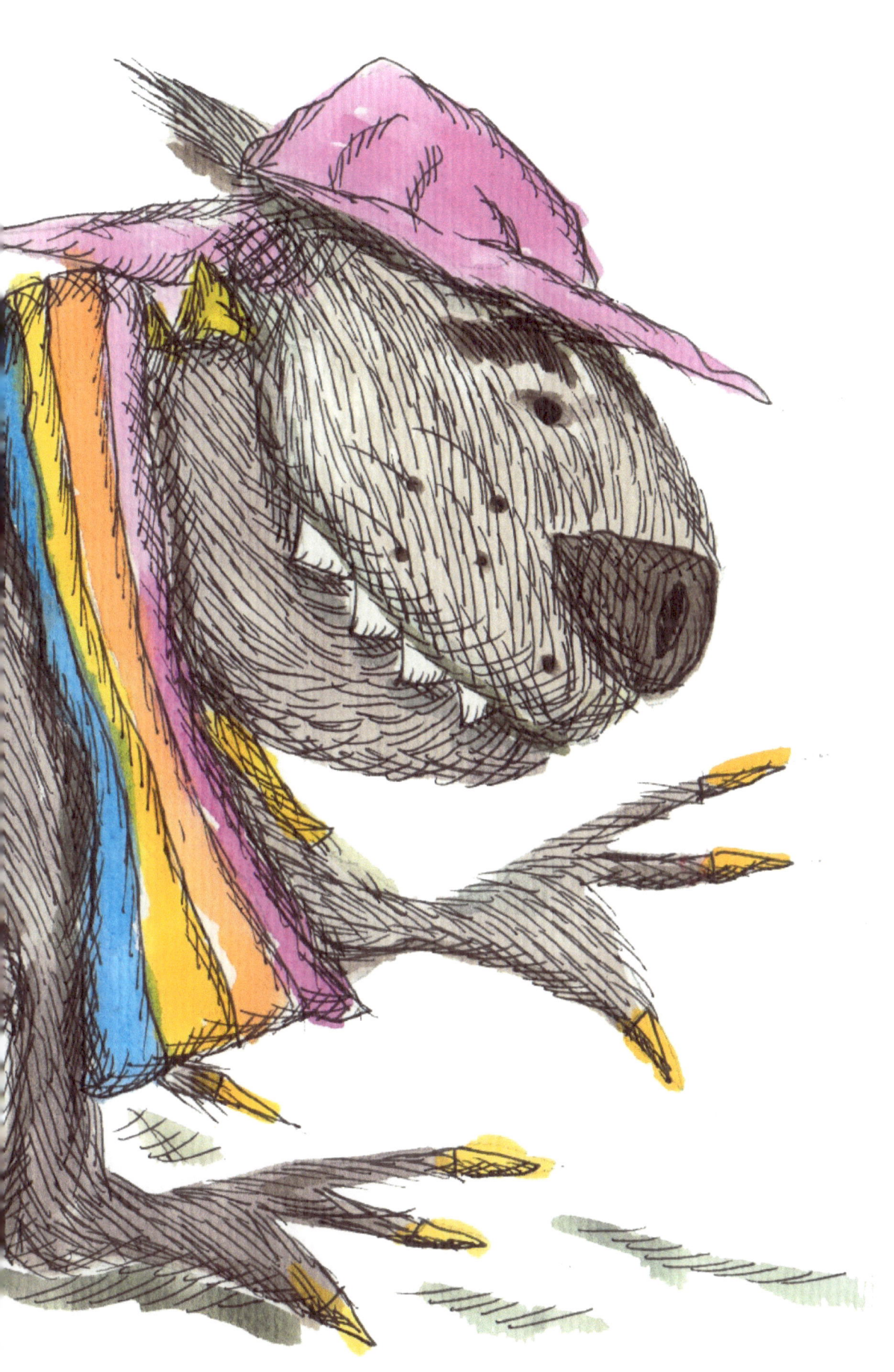

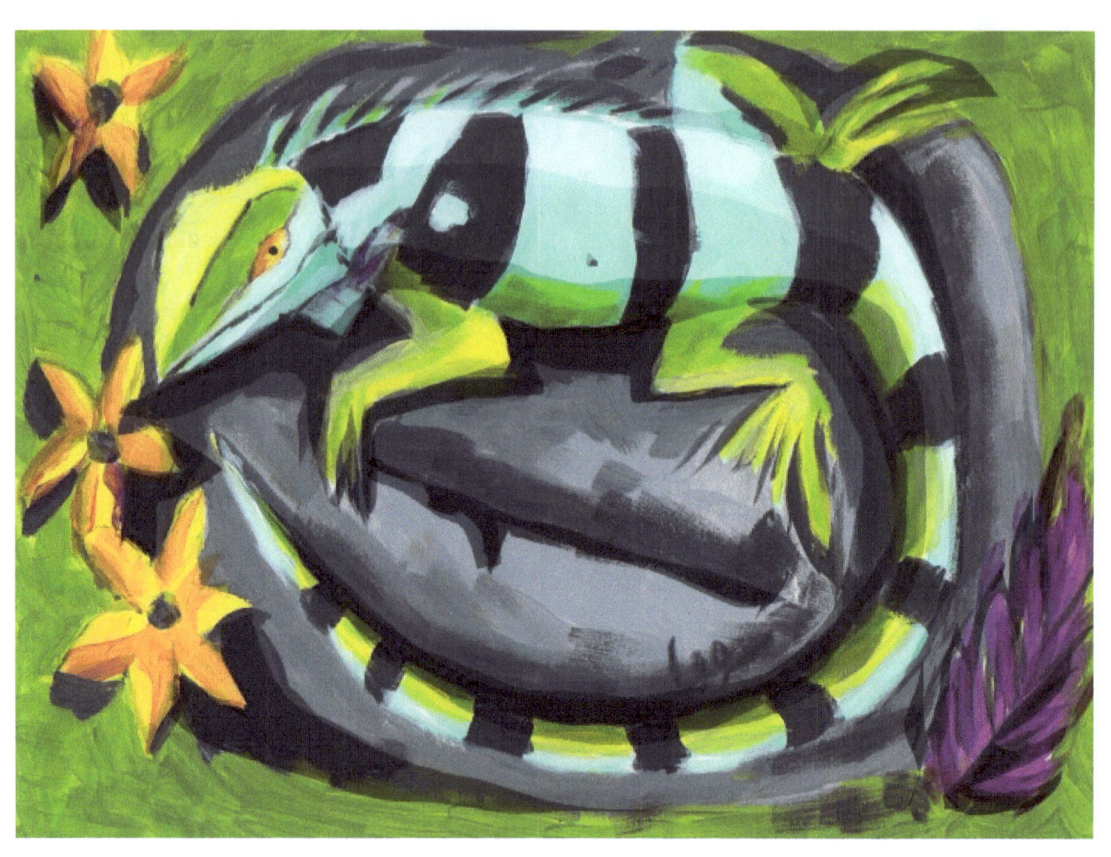

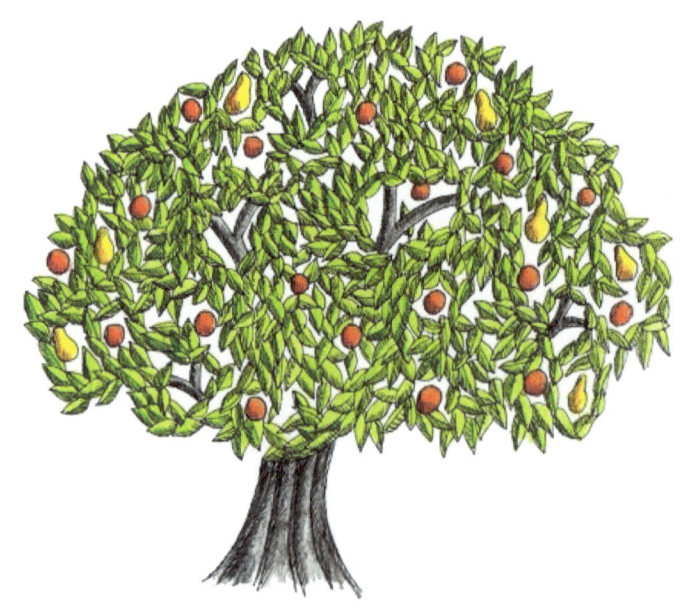

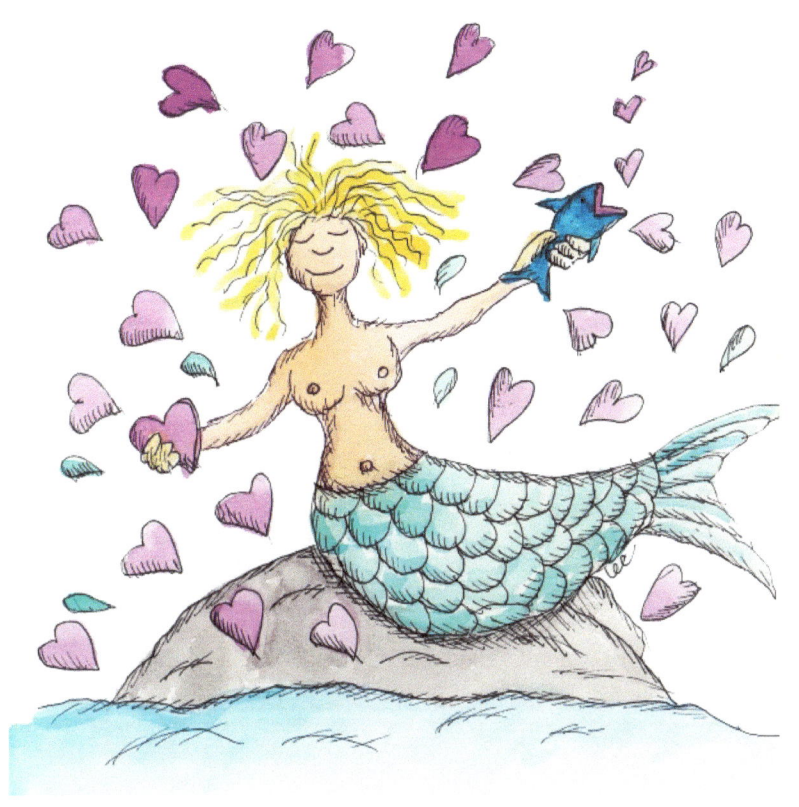

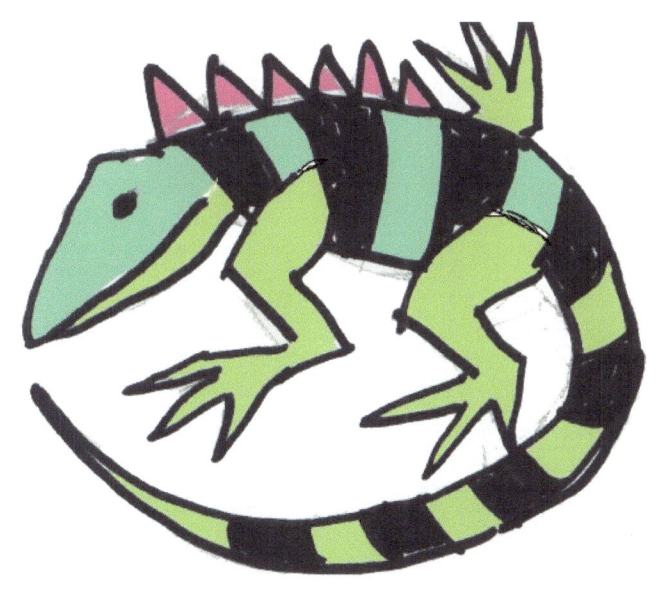

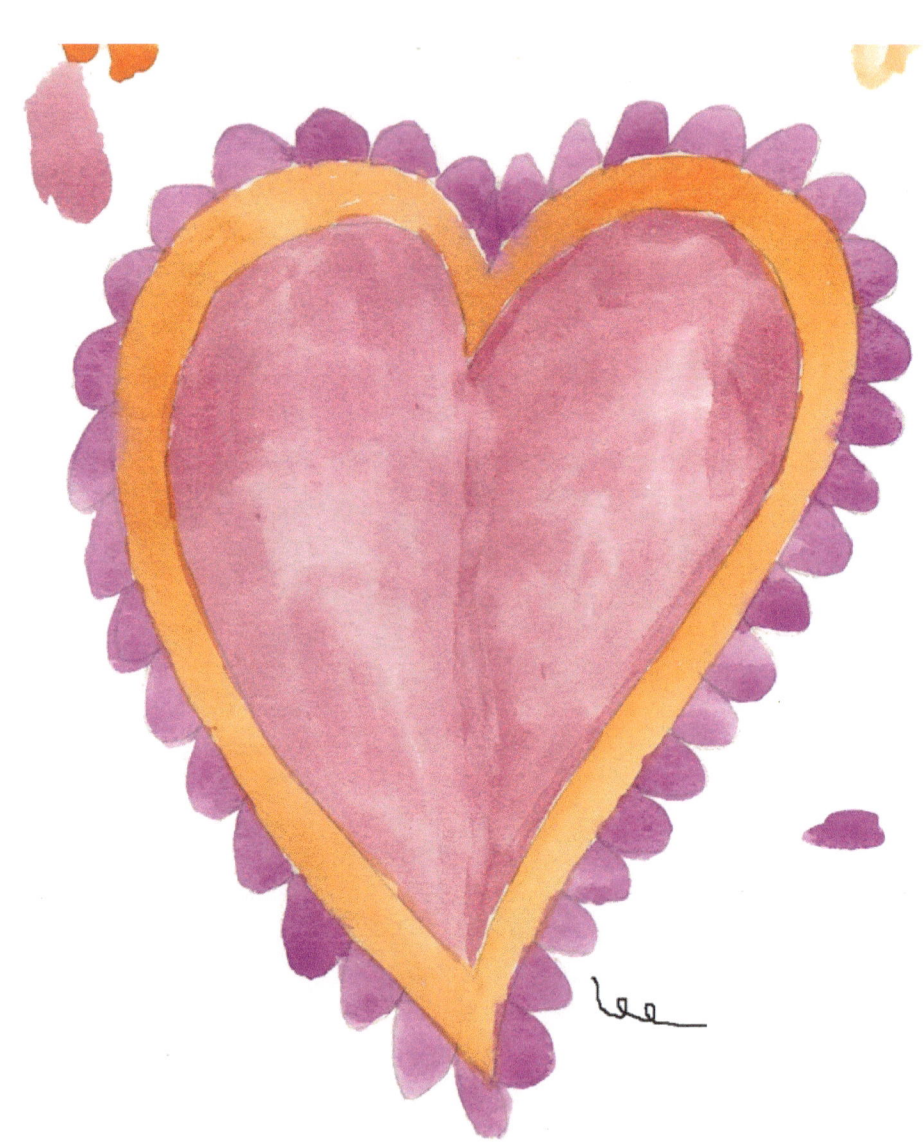

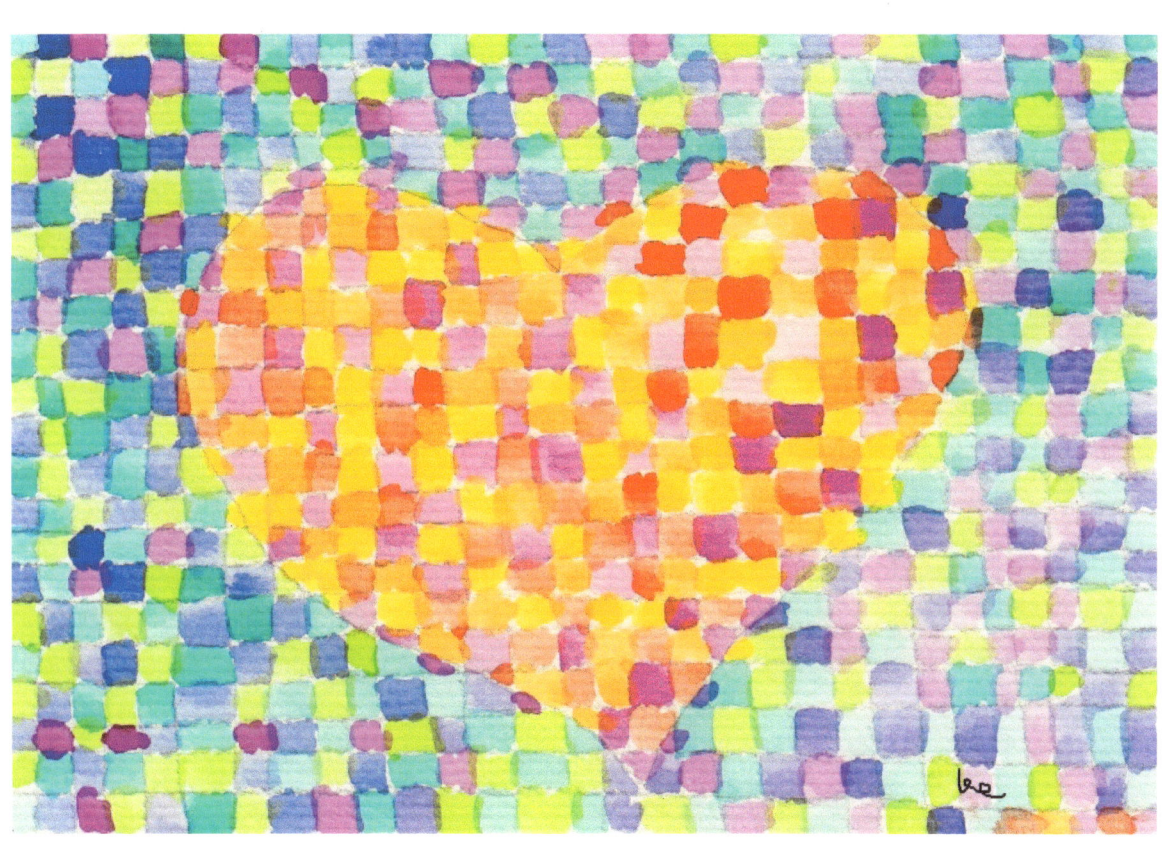

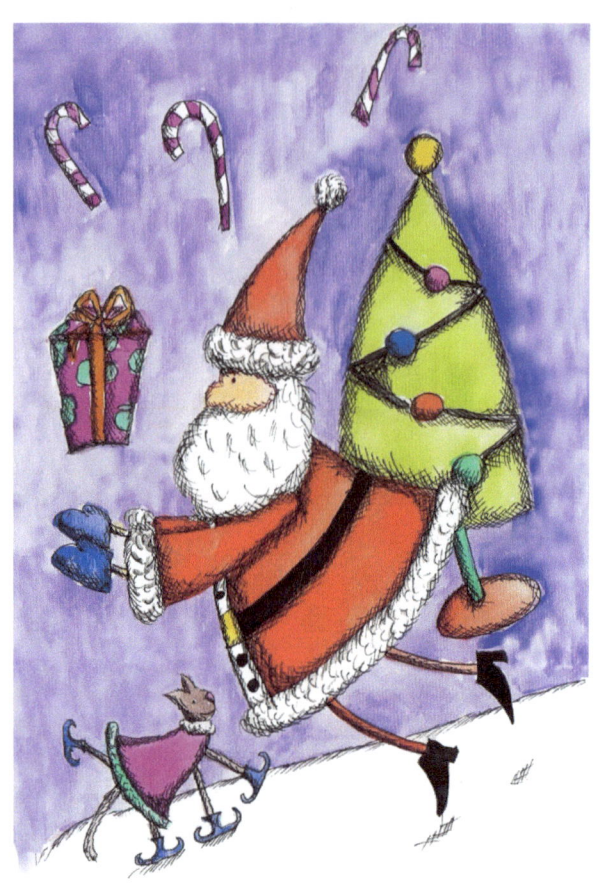

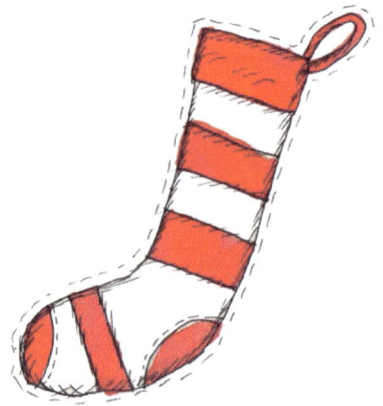

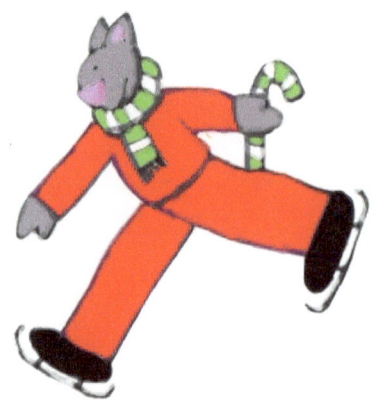

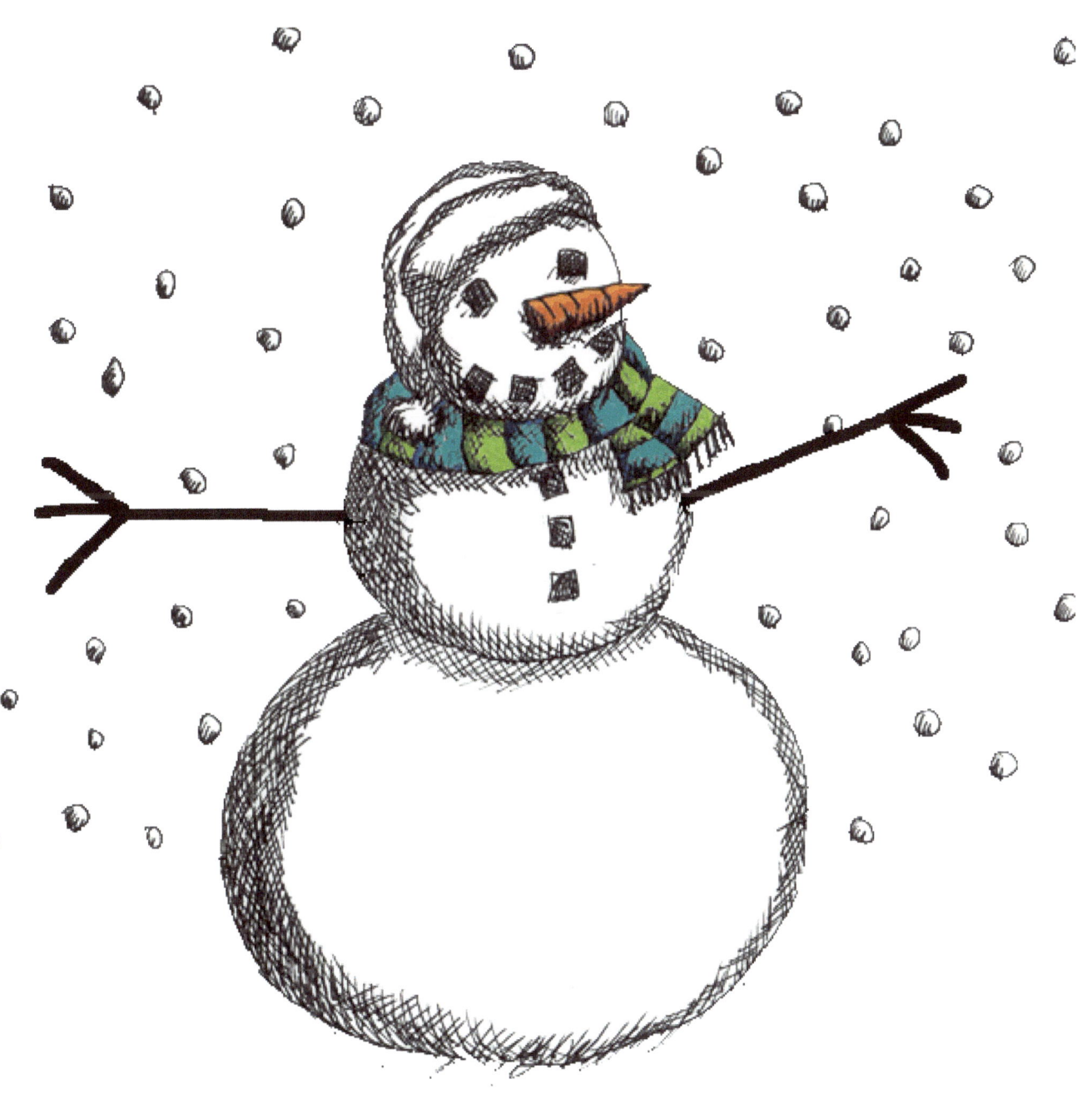

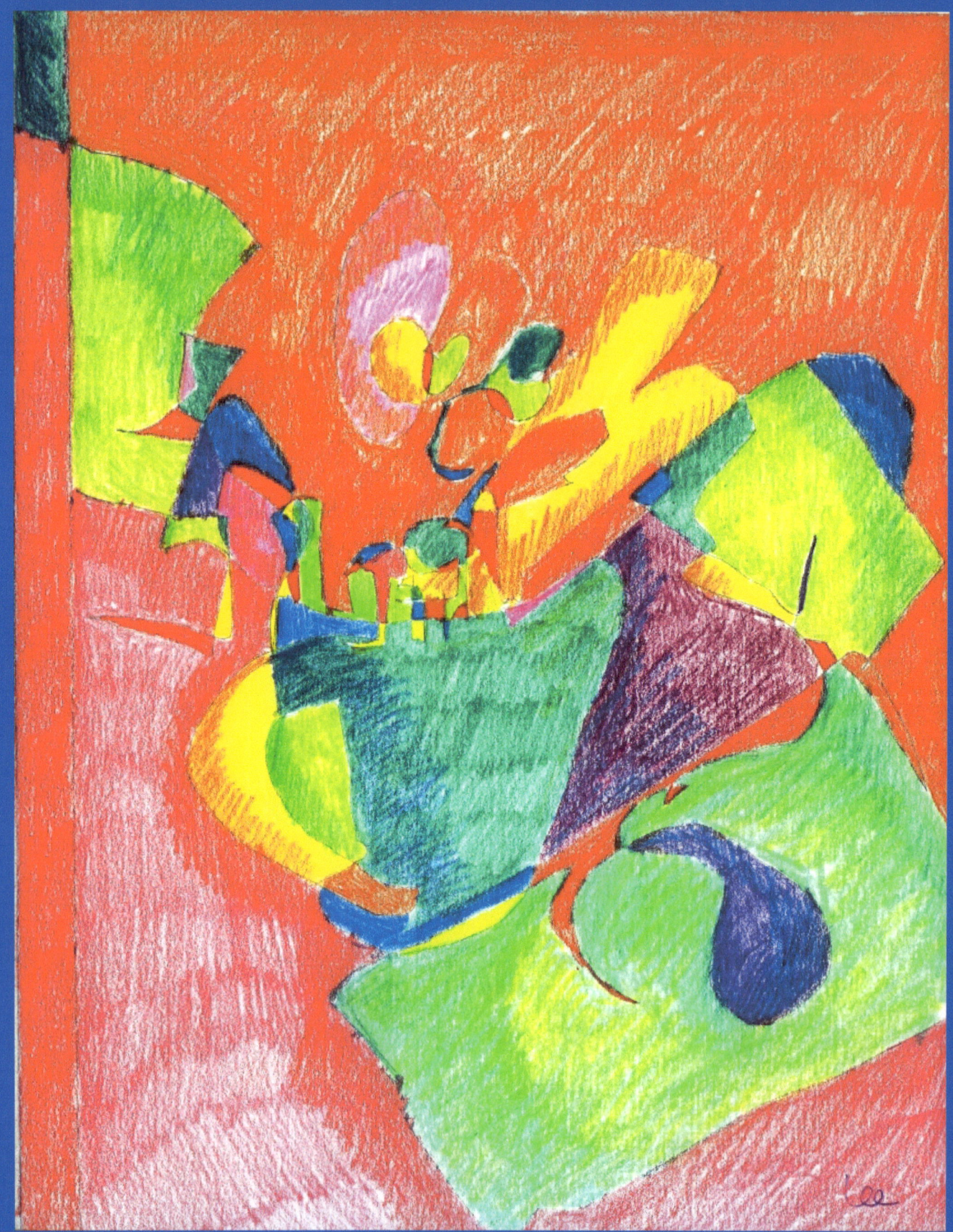

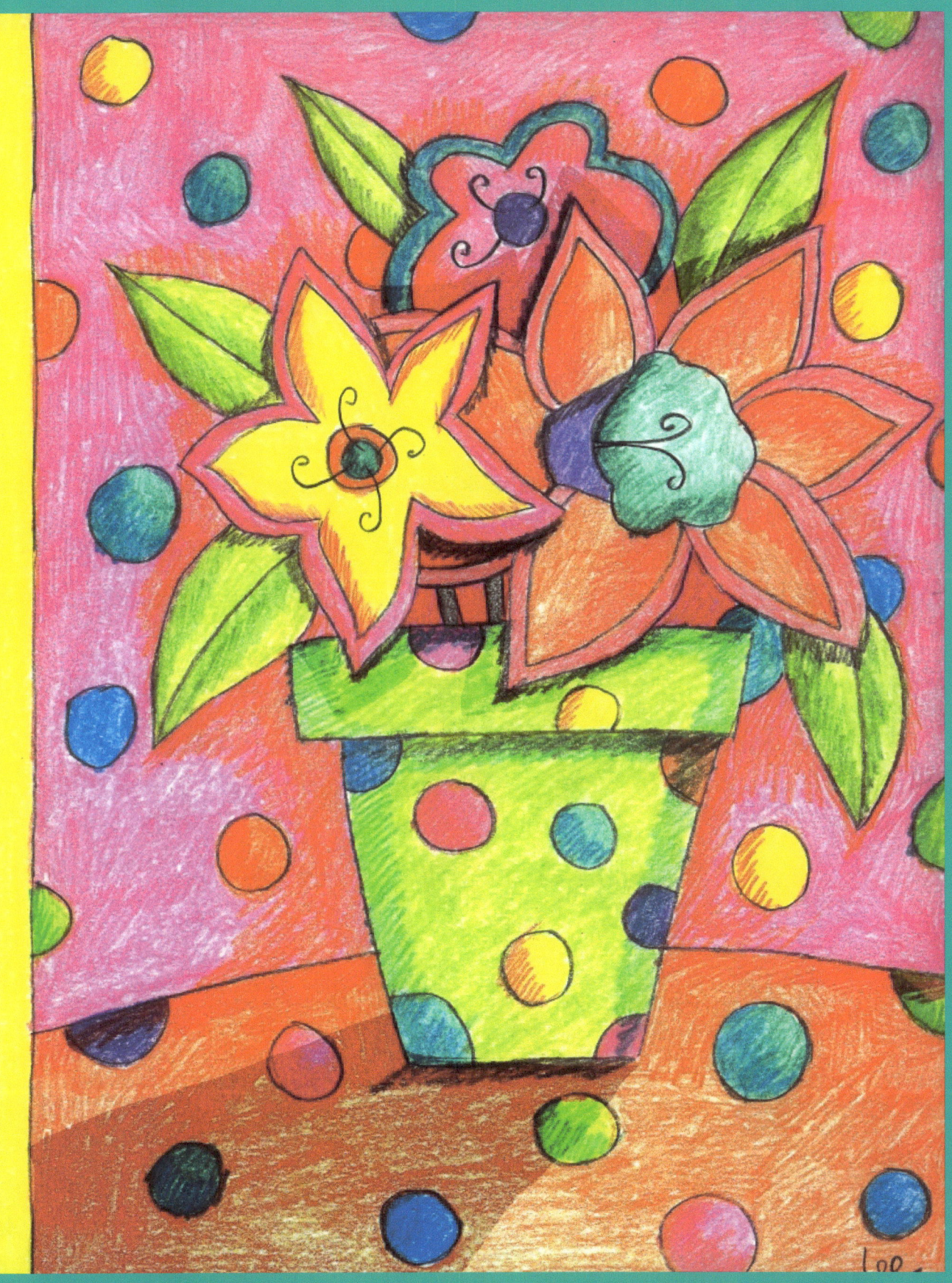

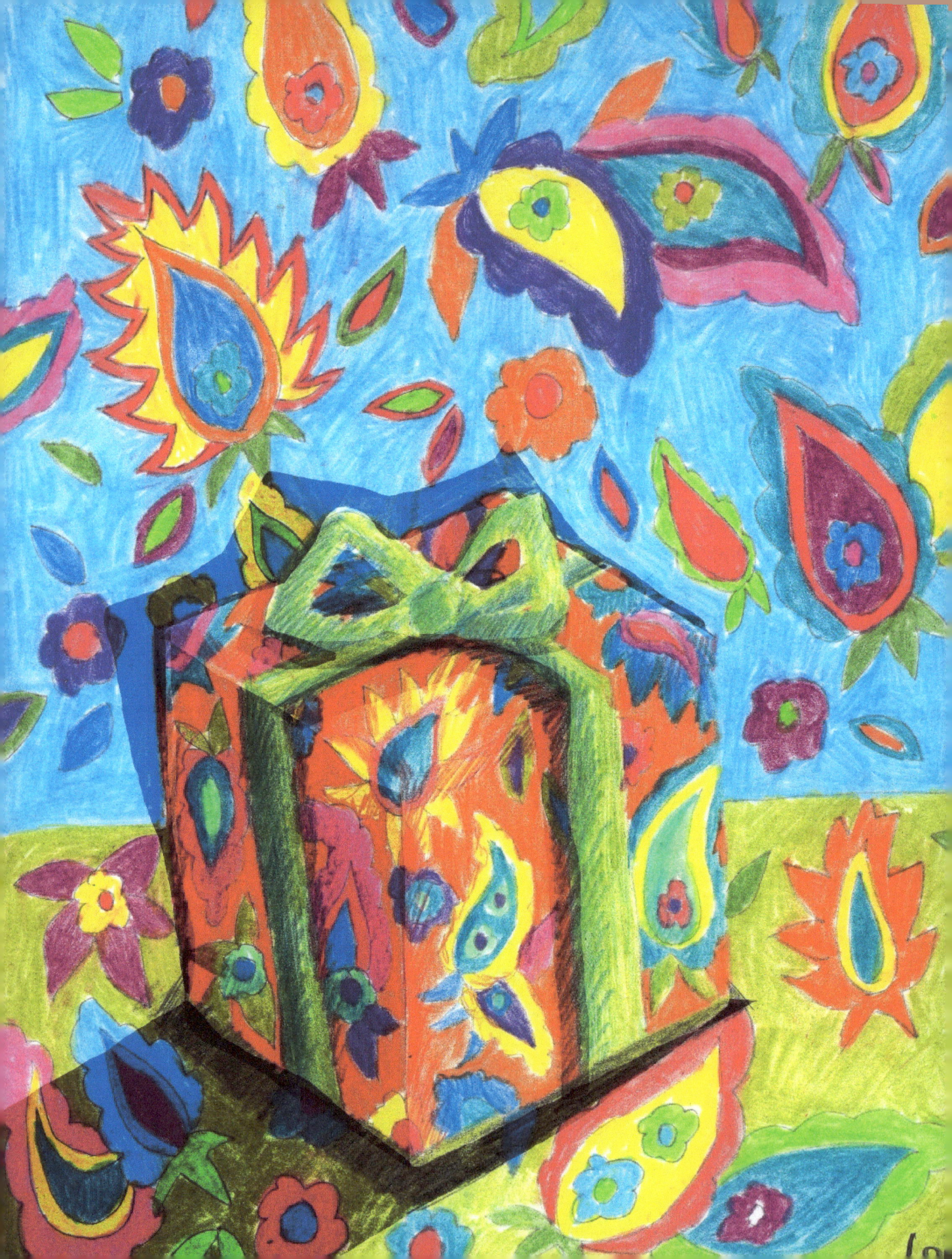

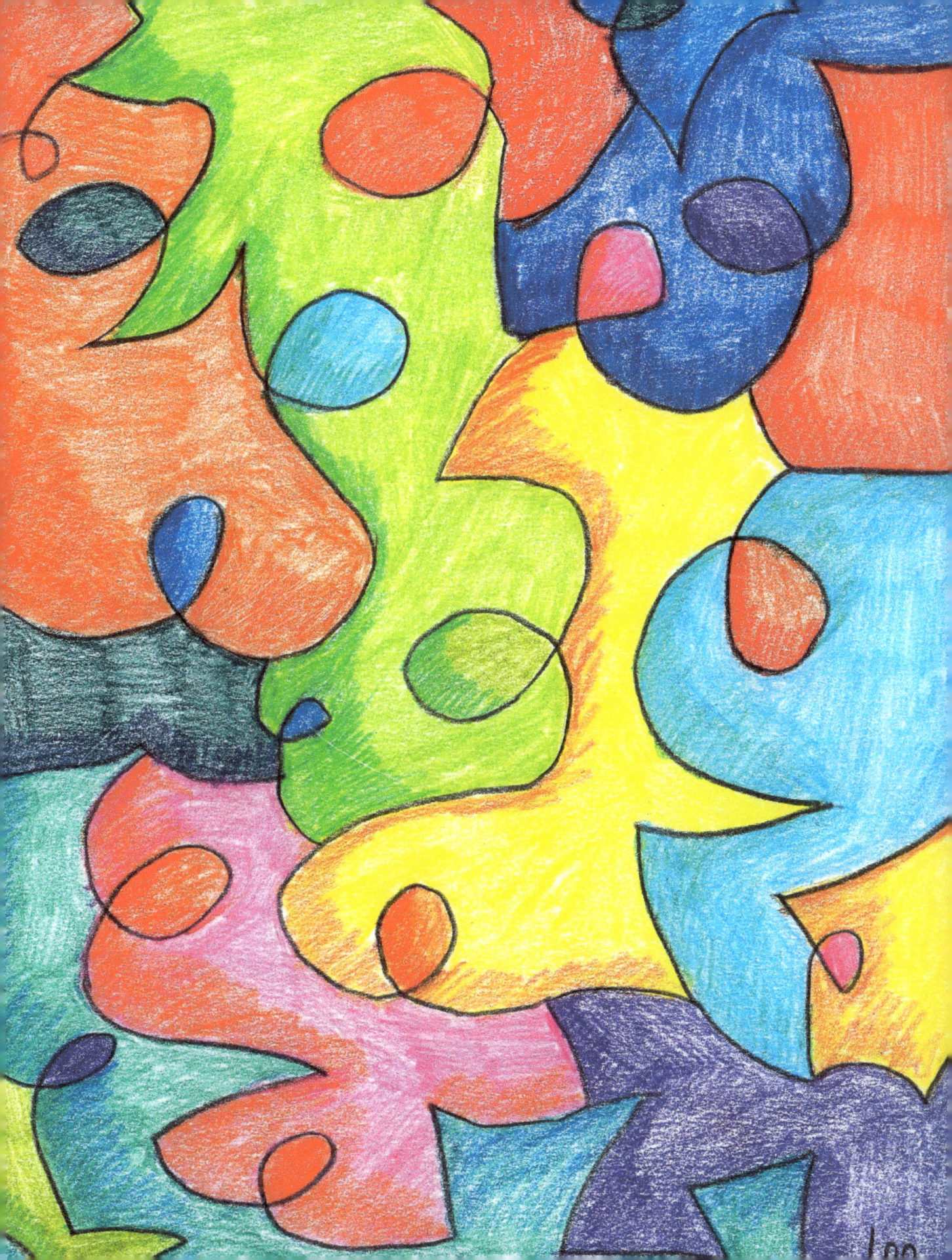

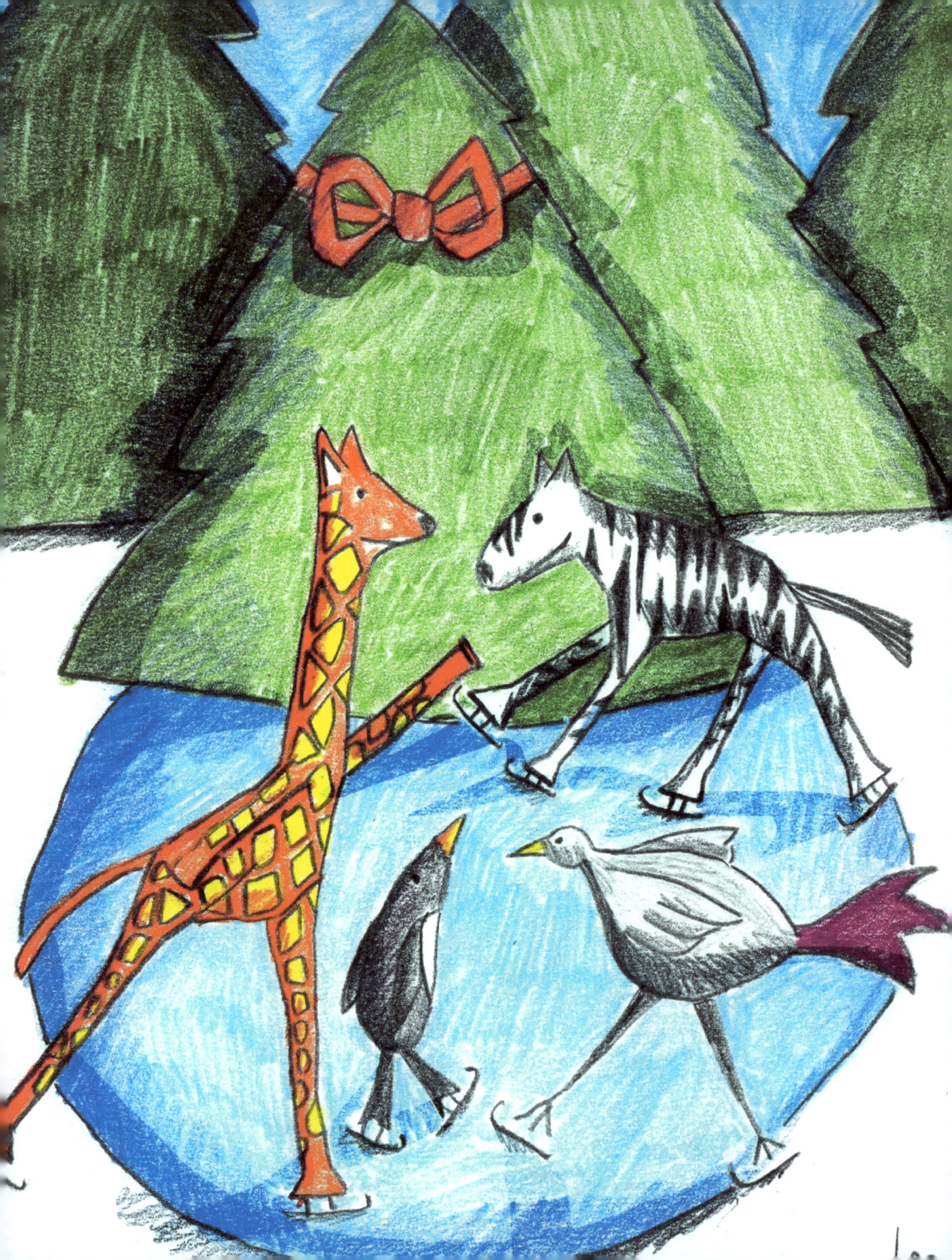

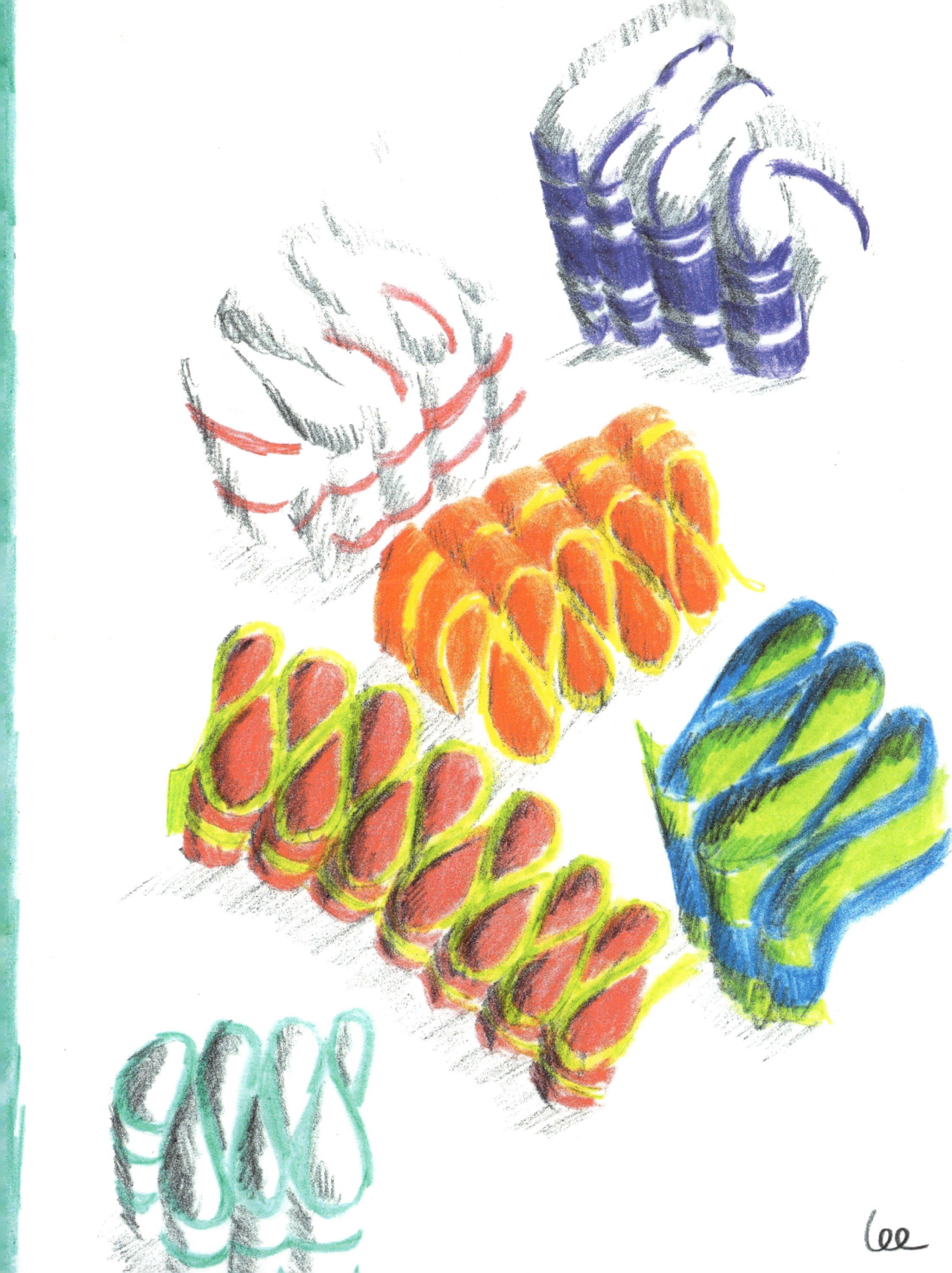

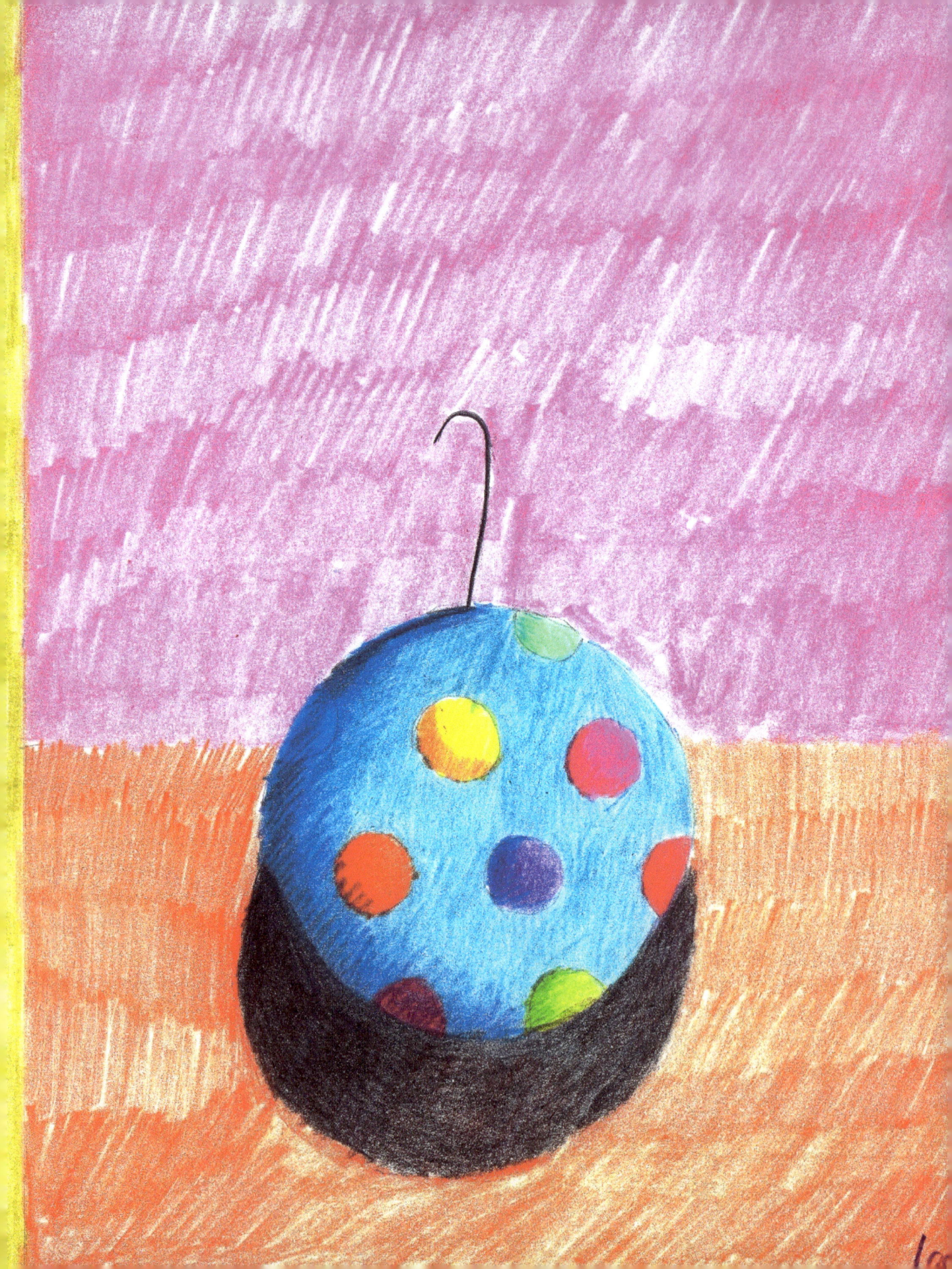

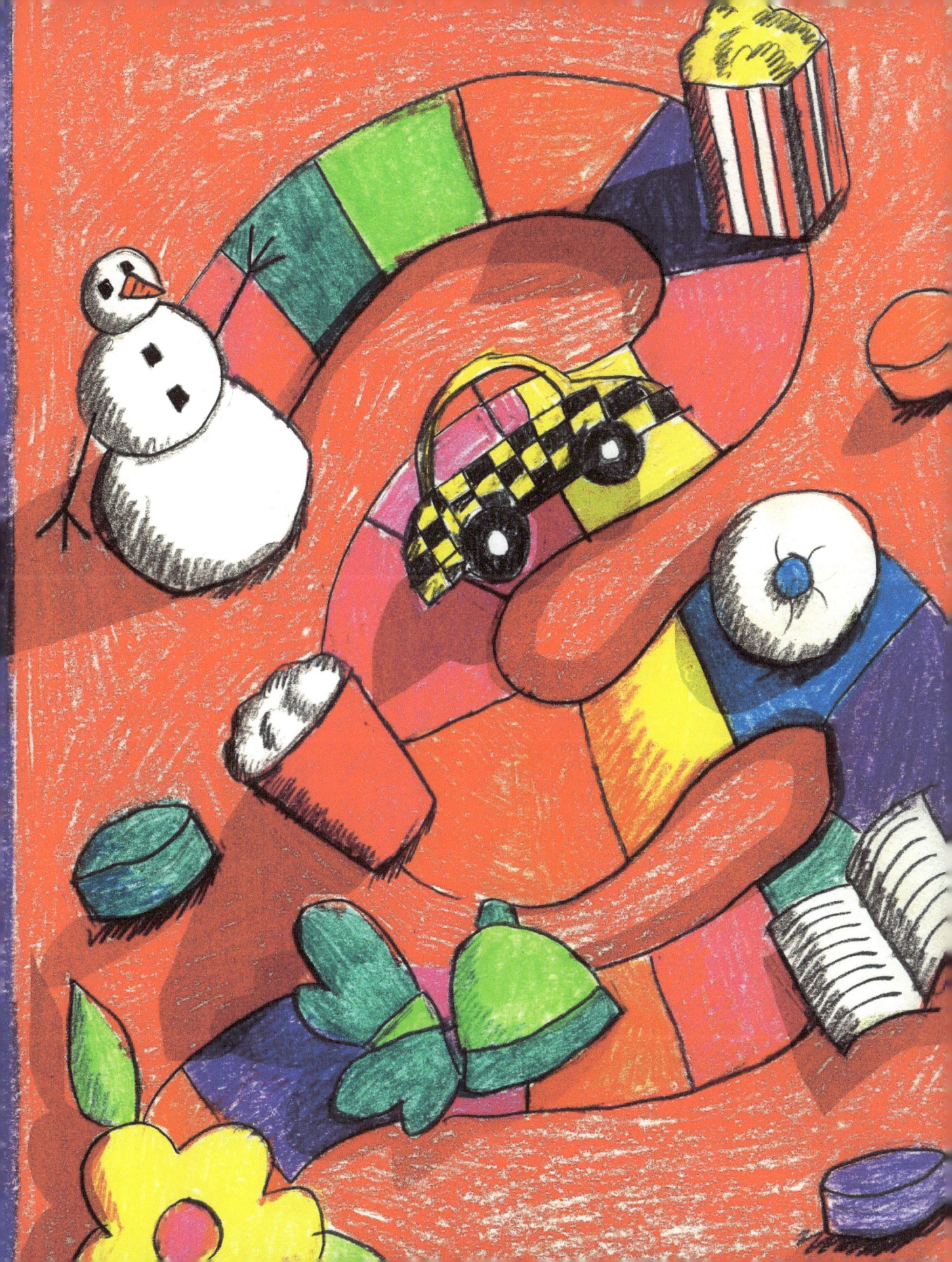

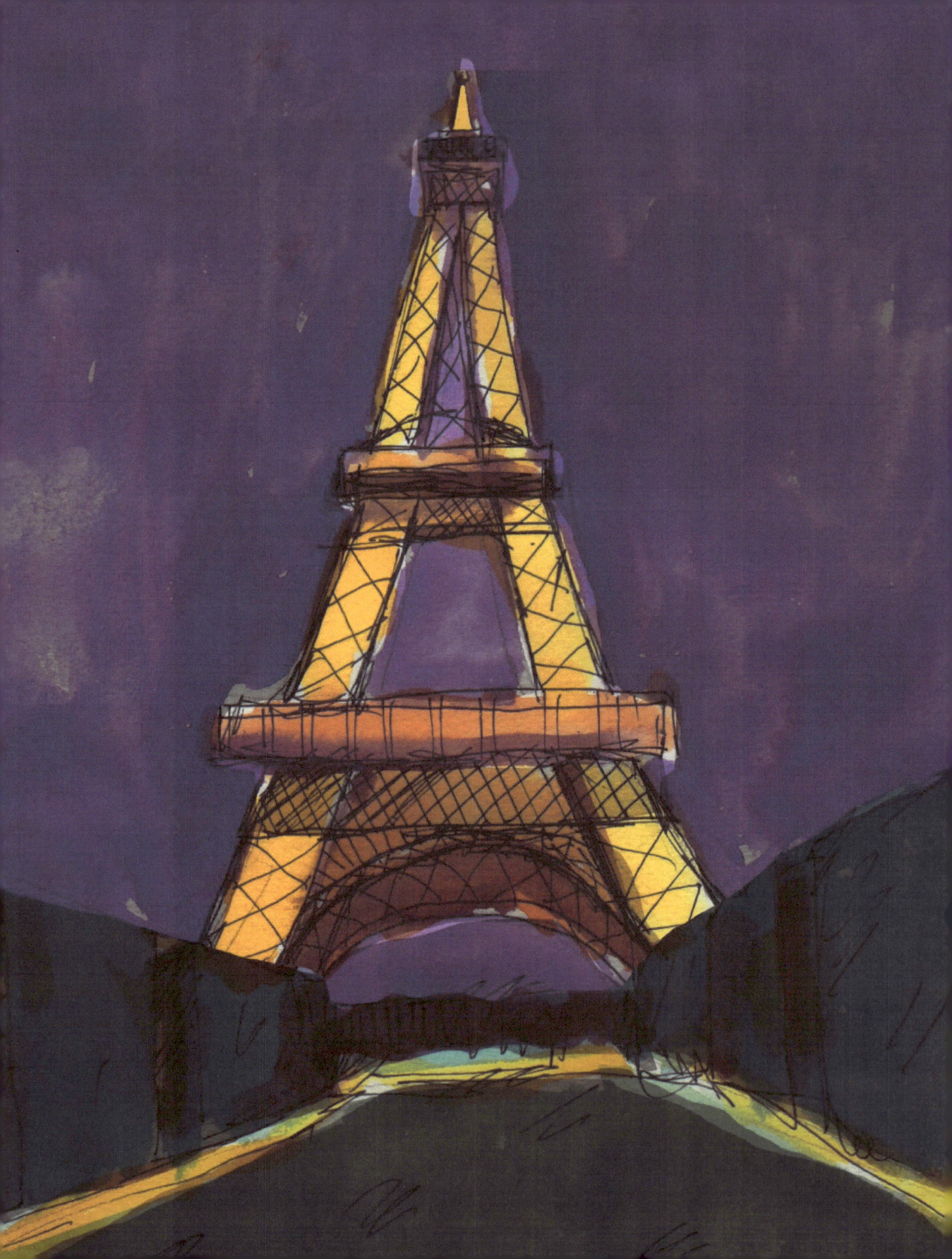

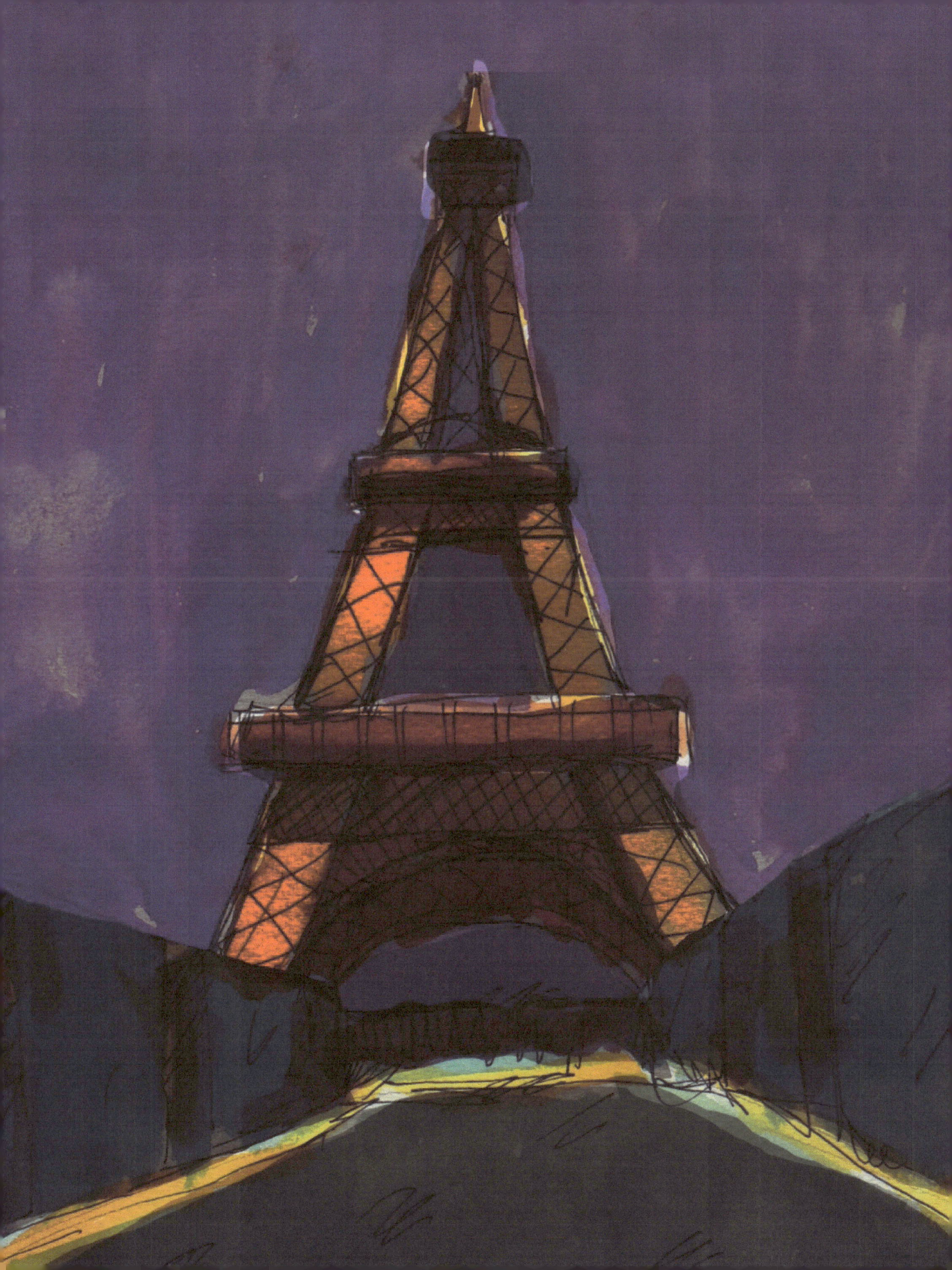

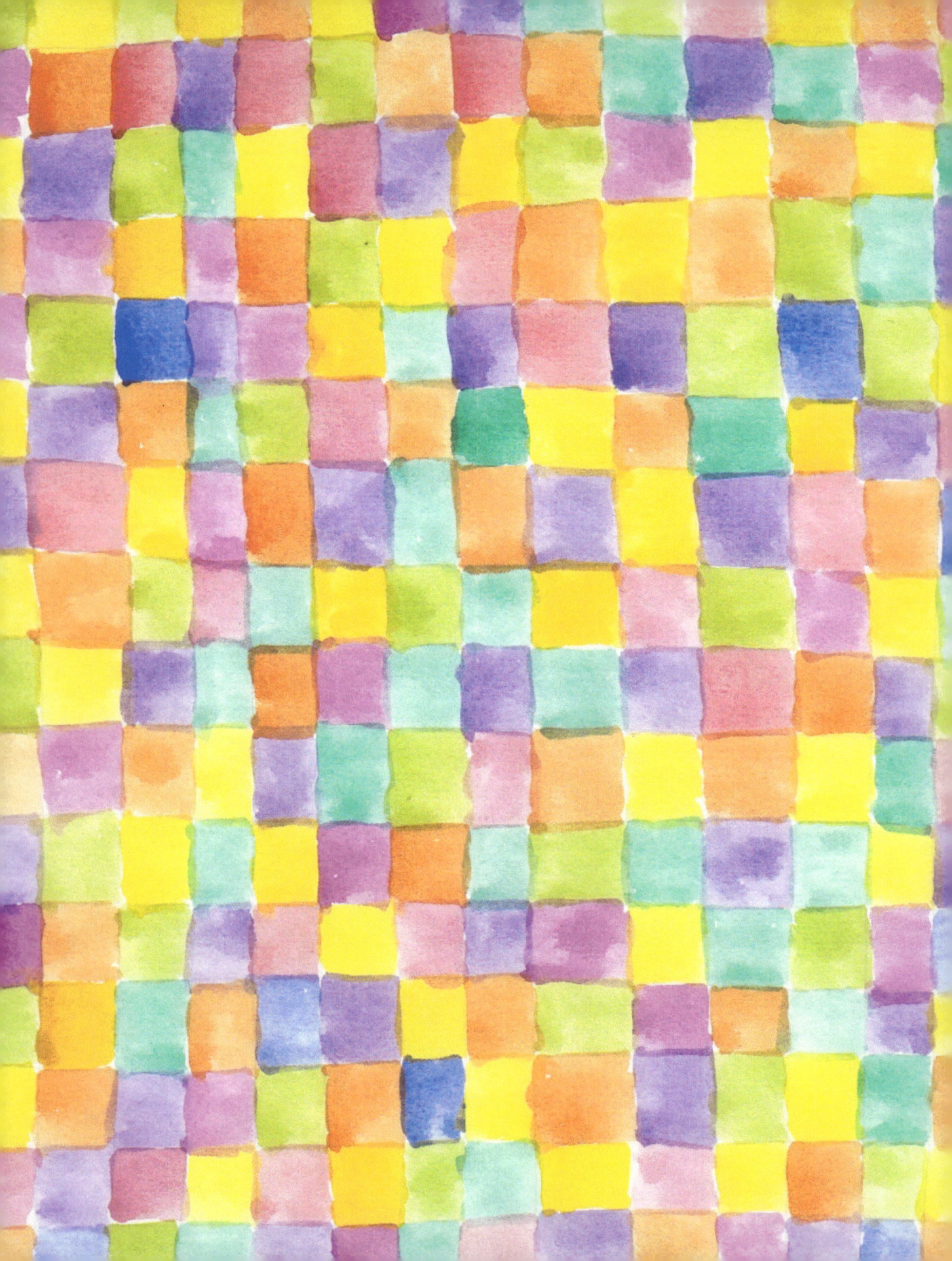

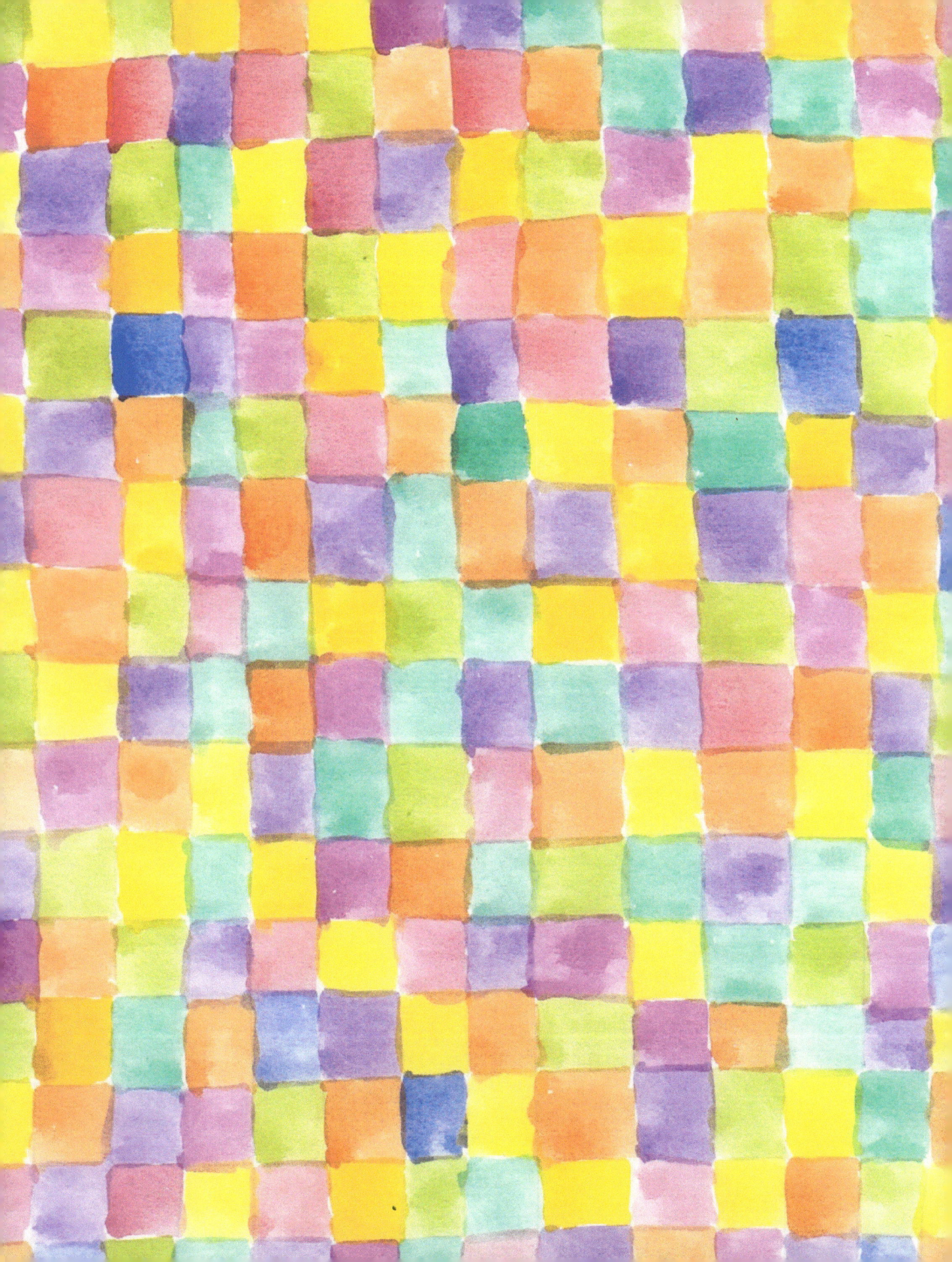

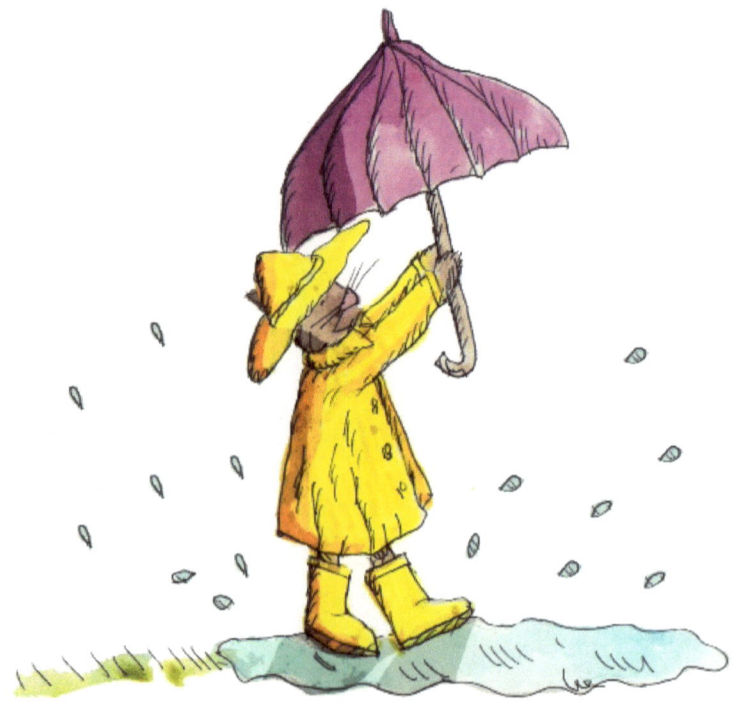

www.ingramcontent.com/pod-product-compliance
Lightning Source LLC
Chambersburg PA
CBHW050858180526
45159CB00007B/2718